To the Notable
Norwood

The
Unspeakable
ADAMS

Phillip Adams (signature)

The
Unspeakable
ADAMS

Phillip Adams

Forty controversial and
popular pieces

Illustrations by John Spooner

Foreword by Alan Marshall

NELSON

Thomas Nelson Australia
480 Latrobe Street Melbourne Victoria 3000

First published 1977
Reprinted 1977 (three times), 1978, 1979, 1981
Copyright © Phillip Adams, 1977
          © John Spooner, illustrations, 1977

Adams, Phillip.
    The unspeakable Adams.
    ISBN 0 17 005178 1
    I. Title.

A824.308

Typeset by Savage and Company, Brisbane
Printed by Tien Mah Litho Printing Co. (Pte) Ltd.

Contents

Foreword
by
Alan Marshall

When first I met Phillip Adams I knew the world in which he roamed would delight me. Maybe his voice and expression were keys to it.

Some years ago I was talking to a swagman I met. He was trying to describe the quality that made a man we both knew a most likeable fellow. He summed up his impression with the remark: 'As soon as he said "Hello", I felt like giving him two bob.' In the case of Phillip Adams I think I would make it a dollar. But the swagman could certainly have been describing a meeting with this charming man.

'Did you read Phillip Adams this morning?' is a question asked by scores of readers with a variety of inflection that suggest their reaction. The reaction varies from uncritical praise to outright hostility. But such responses are inevitable to the work of a satirist. Phillip Adams can be criticized but never ignored.

It is interesting to trace his development as a satirist from his early hilarious articles calculated mainly to rouse laughter, to those in the style of Swift or Voltaire that ridicule our stupidities.

There is no journalist in Australia today who demonstrates the power of the pen more forcibly than Phillip. Certainly his articles reach as many people and have as profound an effect as those of any other satirist in the past. His effect on Australian society has been remarkable. He has ridiculed our weaknesses, mirrored our shortcomings, and attacked our sacred cows. His pointed comments have triggered television programmes, newspaper debates, and inspired soap-box oratory.

Rather than addressing an intellectual élite, he is that modern day phenomenon, a multi-media satirist. Some of the most memorable articles of this remarkable man are collected in this book. The effect of reading them as a collection does not in any way rob them of their spontaneity. Rather it intensifies their impact on all of us who appreciate a clearer view of ourselves.

Alan Marshall

Acknowledgements

The articles contained in this collection first appeared in the *Age* on the following dates, with the exception of 'A personal look at the Fifties', which first appeared in the *Australian*.

'Abyss of eternity' (26 June 1976); 'Cinderella and other tales of subversion' (23 June 1976); 'Why nations go to pot' (29 January 1977); 'The rich are bleeding; ask my chauffeur' (3 July 1974); 'The flag-fall gladiators' (7 February 1976); 'The joyous contraption' (6 November 1976); 'Superfluous Superman' (8 November 1975); 'A schoolboy's language' (12 October 1974); 'Day of the dragon in a child's world' (8 January 1975); 'If these were the best years of our lives, why did we feel so caged?' (15 January 1975); 'Into another dimension' (1 November 1975); 'The film to beat them all' (6 August 1975); 'Disastrous début' (22 January 1977); 'TV or not TV, that's a kwestion' (3 September 1975); 'They're the family drawers' (11 October 1975); 'Of Anzacs and Aztecs' (27 December 1975); 'Around the world in eighty unzips' (5 February 1975); 'Record-breaking among the ruins' (8 February 1975); 'It's time for an old bookworm to turn' (22 December 1976); 'A dog's nose and a maid's knees are always cold' (18 May 1974); 'Baldness seems next to Godliness' (13 November 1976); 'Portrait of an artist scaling the heights' (16 July 1975); 'Somewhere special' (28 February 1976); 'Musings on mortality' (12 June 1976); 'Beating the bumps' (24 December 1976); 'The search for Utopia' (21 September 1974); 'The man in the long white coat...' (28 September 1975); 'The corpse's revenge' (10 March 1976); 'Terror comes cheap at the supermarket' (23 August 1974); 'Peace to all men on dustbin night' (27 November 1974); 'The boys in blue go pink' (19 March 1975); 'The unmaking of a teenage Bolshevik' (30 June 1976); 'The twin religions' (3 July 1976); 'For Christ's sake?' (which appeared originally as 'The ultimate truth') (16 October 1976); 'The shame of the white man' (30 October 1974); 'Lament for a lost lingo' (14 August 1976); 'The journey to Never-Never land' (which appeared originally as 'The journey to death') (19 July 1975); 'A few departing words' (5 October 1974).

The author and publishers would like to thank the staff of the *Age* editorial and pictorial libraries for their help in the compilation of this book.

The extracts on pages 195/6 are taken from *Why I am not a Christian* by Bertrand Russell (Allen & Unwin).

SPOONER.

Abyss of eternity

It's 1944 and I'm five years old, living with my grandparents
in an old weatherboard in what has become a middle-class
suburb of brick veneers with flouncy curtains. Actually,
there are two identical weatherboards, side by side. One for
Grandpa, and the other for his twin brother, Unky. And
although they're hidden from the road by pine trees and
peppercorns, the neighbours say that they're slums, a disgrace to the neighbourhood. Their children, my playmates,
are forever reminding me of our social unacceptability.

Behind the trees and the houses we've four acres of flower
beds. There are violets and poppies and, around Mother's
Day, the white chrysanthemums that Uncle Tobe takes to
the Victoria Market in his ute. There's a stable where we
keep the old draught horse, with its pile of steaming manure
that Grandpa puts on the dahlia beds. And behind it, by
the well, there's a large shed where Grandpa keeps the chaff,
his seed and piles of wooden boxes. It's here, on the dirt
floor, that Grandpa screws up newspapers and burns them,
so as to scorch the stems of his poppies. And every Saturday
night the brothers have singsongs with their cobbers, to the
accompaniment of a small piano and a large quantity of
beer.

My father is at the war. He's a padre, whatever that

1

means. From time to time he gets some leave and this bright yellow man appears (Nan says it's the pills he takes) and gives me some souvenirs, like the bayonet of a dead Japanese soldier or a pair of stone knives made by the Fuzzy-Wuzzies. In between, he sends me coconuts. The postie puts them by the letterbox beneath the peppercorn tree, huge fibrous footballs with 'Master Phillip Adams' carved into their hides, with patriotic postage stamps glued on top. And I don't see much of Mum who lives closer to the city and to her job at a mysterious place called the Rationing.

Grandpa seems as huge, grey and gnarled as the trunk of the peppercorn in which I play Tarzan. Sometimes he lets me plough with him and as I stumble down the furrows beneath his arms, it's like taking part in a creation with God. Twenty years hence I'll find some old Box Brownie photographs and realise that he and Unky were quite short. It was just that they felt big.

He's always gruff with me but I sense that it's like the thick crust on warm bread. The bread he hacks into wedges at breakfast while sitting at the linoleum-topped table with The *Age* propped up on a bottle of Nan's tomato sauce. He grunts his way through the news but always remembers to hand me the page with Curly Wee on it. While on Sunday mornings he makes me breakfast, either a monstrous sandwich of corned beef suppurating in sauce, with a piece of string trailing from the bread, or else some toast and dripping. Which he brings to my sleepout under the peppercorns. 'Here y'are, Cockel', he says, clomping over the bare boards in his hobnails.

I don't think Grandpa ever speaks more than a dozen words a day to me, but when he dies, ten years later, it will be the greatest loss I've ever known. I'll visit him in the hospital, in his last hours, to confront a whimpering, shrunken thing that cannot, *must* not be the same man. And I'll try desperately to remember him harnessing Blossom or tossing mallee roots from the ute, one in each hand. Or standing

2

by the piano singing *The Old Rugged Cross* in a manner worthy of his beloved Peter Dawson. His death will come very shortly after age and illness force him to sub-divide and sell the land, so that forty brick veneers can be built on his flower beds.

I'll always remember the excitement of the auction, performed in a marquee, and I will be shocked when I subsequently learn that the auctioneer was a crook, and that Grandpa and his brother were robbed of thousands and thousands of pounds. After forty-five years of work, fifty years if you count the time they spent at the goldfields, Bill and Fred Smith will have to humble their pride and take the pension.

My sleepout is beneath the peppercorns and the pines. I'm almost lost in Grandma's old brass bed and have a crystal set beside me on a ricketty bamboo table. But just as often I prefer to listen to the wind in the trees or the rain on the galvo. And perhaps because I'm living with old people, I think about dying. I wonder what it will feel like to be dead.

Will I *know* I'm dead? Will I be able to think? Will I have memories? Will I lie there, in the grave, feeling the slow passing of the endless days, or will a hundred years seem like a second? Or will it be nothingness? And if so, what colour is nothingness? Black or white? I push my face into the pillow and see colours swirling up in the darkness, and I feel myself falling into the night, through the trees and the clouds, beyond the reach of the wartime searchlights, past the Moon and the stars, until there's only darkness and a vast emptiness. And still I fall, falling *upwards* in a vastation of terror. Of *mortal* terror. For I realise that eternal space and the eternal time of death are one and the same thing. That both go on and on forever and that neither can have an end.

And yet they must. Nothing can go on without stopping. Everything must have a beginning and an ending. The

3

thought of eternity is so awesome that I feel a sort of orgasmic dread that chills every atom. So I sit up in bed and fumble for the lamp, wincing in its sudden glare and saying over and over to myself that 'I'm Phillip Adams and live at 798 High Street, East Kew', using the light to block out the ultimate darkness and those pitiful pieces of data to protect me from the reality of the abyss.

Night after night I know the same consternation and despair. I ask Nan about infinity who assures me that there was a beginning and that the beginning was God. But she's impatient with me when I ask the inevitable question 'But who began God?'

Her view of the universe seems lopsided and illogical, for she insists on a beginning but cannot accept an end. So on the one hand she has a creation while on the other there's a never-ending heaven. To me that seems as silly and unbalanced as a one-sided see-saw and, try as I might, I cannot take God seriously. I *yearn* to believe in Him, so that He could end the nightmares that prevent me sleeping. But when I fall upwards into the sky, tumbling through the stars, I find no evidence of His heaven let alone of His presence. All I experience is emptiness and meaninglessness.

Finally I can stand it no more. There *has* to be an end to space, so that there can be an end to time, to the millions of centuries of death. So one night I invent a rocky vault around space, a vault that contains everything from the stars and the Sun to the world and my fear. And for a while I'm reassured. The panic is stilled.

But inevitably, there comes a night when despite my attempts to clutch at the bed and at my chanted litany of name and address, I find myself falling once more. And in my mind's eye I see my sleepout in High Street, in Kew, in Melbourne, in Victoria, in Australia, in the Southern Hemisphere, the World and the Universe. The very same concentric listing that kids are forever writing on the front of their exercise books.

4

Now, as I pass the final stars, I know I'm about to put my rocky vault to the test. Which, of course, it fails. For this time it's as fragile as eggshell and I crash through it to discover that there's even more space beyond. In that second, I resign to my fate of being a finite being in an infinite, indifferent void. And all the prayers and sermons of my father who art in New Guinea or his Father Who art in Heaven, will never change that certainty.

As for my infrequent visits to Sunday school, they only serve to make religion seem ridiculous.

I might enjoy Superman comics and Captain Marvel but how can I accept stories of miraculous healings, of conjuring food for a multitude from a few loaves and fishes, or walking on water? To me these are the desperate fantasies of people who cannot face their loneliness in space and time.

Soon the war is over but my parents are not reunited. From the sleepout, I can hear the raised voices in the good room that Nan hardly ever uses. Only for very special occasions like a wake, or, as it turns out, the end of a marriage. I learn that there's to be a divorce and both parents take me aside and tell me that I'll have to stand up in a courtroom and make a choice between them. For months on end I agonise over the prospect. Finally, I'm spared both the courtroom and the decision as it's decided I'll stay with my grandparents and will see Mum and Dad at weekends.

About this time Unky decides to leave his house behind the pines and to move in with his married daughter. So they sell one of the identical weatherboards to the cemetery trust. I see it being jacked up and lowered onto a truck and am allowed to ride a little way up High Street. To move along the tram tracks in a house is a remarkable sensation. Then, after a two-mile trip that stops what little traffic there was in 1946, it's dragged into the Kew Cemetery. They have to dismantle and rebuild a large section of the brick fence to complete the job and, for years after, you can see where the cement is a different colour. The house is still there today

5

and what seemed a big building to me as a kid is revealed as a tiny working man's cottage.

After Unky's departure and the formal burial of his house, it is decided to sub-divide. So a man comes and shoots the draught horse because there's nowhere to keep him. Every paddock for miles has, almost overnight, been covered with houses. I hide in the sleepout while that terrible job is being done, refusing to emerge until the carcase has been carted away. Even then I can't avoid the bright blood on the grass and stare at it in disbelief and fascination. Whereupon the local agent, a man well known in church and civic circles, holds his auction and knocks down the blocks at bargain prices to his mates in the crowd. Within a year one block will be resold for as much as the brothers got for ten. Soon Grandpa is ailing and dying, and it's my job to break the news to Nan, sitting rocking and sobbing on the edge of her bed.

Within the year, people have planted their prissy shrubs and garden gnomes where Grandpa had grown his 'chrissies'. However, Nan and I live on in the little house and the sleepout, while a little of the pine hedge survives along with my solitary peppercorn. All this time, I find myself thinking about death, trying to find some sense of the non-sense of a life with neither destiny or purpose. This drives me from my Superman comics to books, which I read obsessively, becoming more and more solitary.

I'd started school at the time of Hiroshima and Nagasaki and, as a child of those times, my nickname was Adambomb. While the Second World War becomes first a memory and then a myth, there's talk of a Cold War, or a third world war with nuclear weapons that will be over within hours. So I belong to a generation that grows up beneath the spectre of a mushroom cloud and inevitably these fears reinforce my own anxieties, until I can see no future. I look at people building homes or wheeling prams with a mixture of pity and disgust. Don't they read the papers or listen to the news? Don't they realise that even if they lived to finish their houses, their children will never grow up?

While clearly I feel these things more deeply than my friends, all kids I know feel some intimations of doom. To a large extent, this explains the sudden emergence of the teenager as a distinct entity with his own culture. Even if it were subconscious, we think we're unlikely to live to be twenty let alone thirty. So we insist on the right to live more intensely in whatever time is left. I remember the theme from *Blackboard Jungle, Rock Around the Clock*, serving as our Marseillaise in the noisy revolution which follows. At the same time, Spike Milligan and his Goons give us an absurdist philosophy that's far more help in coping with the monstrous illogicality of the Arms Race than anything we'd heard in church.

Well, twenty years have passed and the world hasn't come to an end. At least, not yet. Yet our children face even more apocalyptic threats, have dozens of doomsdays to contemplate. While waiting for the nuclear bombs to fall they hear the population explosions with the attendant talk of growing crises in energy and food. There's the mushroom cloud of cancer and the constant discussion of ecological disasters.

At the same time, we've grown accustomed to living under threat, to accepting our Damoclean situation as matter-of-factly as Londoners coping with their terrorist bombings.

Nonetheless, we and our children still live with death. It's as vivid and omnipresent to us as it was the plague-ridden Middle Ages. And this is still reflected in teenage culture, in the manic energy that says 'We want everything *now*,' in the growing acquiescence to drugs and in the headlong rush to any self-appointed, self-annointed Messiah who happens along. At the same time, the philosophic implications of death remain undiscussed. While subjects like sex are discussed to death, death itself remains taboo.

My grandfather's house was sold shortly after Nan died. It was promptly dismantled along with my bungalow and an axe was taken to the surviving trees. But for some reason it has remained empty for almost a decade, the only vacant block in the district of what are now middle-aged houses. I walked around it a few weeks back and found shards of Nan's willow pattern pressed into the dirt while a couple of down-trodden flowers were all that was left from Grandpa's efforts. I then drove to his brother's house, hemmed in behind the cemetery wall; a disgrace to the neighbourhood of marble statuary, those giant chess pieces with which Christians try to play death at his own game. And I realise that I'd long since come to terms with meaninglessness, that I no longer feared death but simply resented it. Because I've come to love life so intensely.

A personal look at the Fifties

I was never any good at languages – not French, not Latin and most certainly not poetry, to me the most foreign tongue of all.

Where most prose writers strive to be lucid, poets prefer to work in the most secret ciphers. Thus I've viewed poetry with the same awe as chess; as a pastime of admirable elegance and total incomprehensibility.

That is, until I read Dylan Thomas, the one poet whose privacy I've managed to invade. He was almost obligatory among my friends, along with records of Josh White, Lottie Lenya and Bessie Smith. Along with black Sobranie cigarettes and the films of Eisenstein. Along with plays of Samuel Beckett and Tennessee Williams. Along with duffel coats, Vespas and Lambrettas. Along with rooms lit by candles stuck in Chianti or Benedictine bottles.

Thomas had recently died from the drink and poetic self-pity, so he was to us what Bryon or Rupert Brooke had been to earlier generations.

> It was my thirtieth year to heaven
> woke to my hearing from harbour
> and neighbour wood
> and the mussel pooled and heron
> priested shore.

When I first read those lines from October Poem they both pained and moved me. My thirtieth birthday was still fourteen years away yet, suddenly, Thomas' words made it seem a memory. Not only had I lived those years already but, worse, they seemed all but forgotten. As I looked into my future I felt not curiosity but sadness and nostalgia. I was overwhelmed with the poignancy of youth and the remorselessness of time.

From romanticism to rheumatism. I found that poem again today, and it pained and moved me still. For now my thirtieth year from heaven is a memory, along with my thirty-first, thirty-second and thirty-third. But at the same time I was glad to read it, because it brought back my Fifties in extraordinary vivid detail. It was very different to be young then. I was moving from the bodgies to the bolshies while, at the same time, being drawn to Bohemia as it was understood by the Melbourne of Menzies era.

Bohemia. What an old-fangled word it sounds in the era of obligatory permissiveness when women's magazines are concerned more with orgasm than organza. And even then it was pretty tame, its élitist fantasies contracting with the egalitarianism of today's drop-outs.

Exhibit A. In our circle, films meant small-screen, sub-titled, black-and-white, demanding films. In an act of cultural as well as political commitment, I'd got the job of screening Russian classics at the New Theatre in Flinders Street, trying to synchronise Shostakovich 76s with the Odessa steppes sequence. Or Rimsky-Korsakov with the childhood of Maxim Gorky (The Cold War was at its coldest, the commercial cinema shunning movies from the Eastern bloc, and ASIO tapping our phone.) And had we been told that ten years hence intelligent filmgoers would abandon the art film in favour of B-features and westerns we wouldn't have believed it.

Any more than we'd have believed the ability of Christianity to resurrect itself. It's true that my left-wing activities branded me as mildly eccentric, given that most of my friends were totally apolitical, preferring to express their disaffection in other ways (such as by singing *The Threepenny Opera* and putting candles in those Chianti bottles). But we all agreed that religion was in its last gasps, that the future belonged to reason and, with qualification, to science.

While some of the group flirted with seances or dianetics, most were drawn to the existentialism of Sartre and Camus. Existentialism. What a wonderful, satisfying word. It was almost as if you were transformed by merely pronouncing it, if I could pronounce it. It was as if it was an intellectual counterpart of 'Shazam.'

We took our art very seriously too, going the rounds of galleries and worrying about abstract versus figurative. I can well remember the long arguments we had with painters we knew, with us insisting they move away from mythic, mulga themes (Aboriginals, bushrangers and explorers) so as to paint Holdens and neon signs.

Subsequently the pop art movement would've gained our approval, but we'd have been uneasy about the mass-produced posters that provide today's trendy decor. Like the unpredictable enthusiasm from American movies it would've seemed excessive, overly democratic, a denial of standards.

Standards. We certainly had those, ridiculous as they might seem with the cynicism of hindsight. For example, in sexual matters we had a rough rule of thumb, or penis, that approved of pre-marital or extra-marital encounters provided they involved 'affection'. By and large we weren't ready to condone out-and-out promiscuity. The gravitational pull of Melbourne's middle-class morality was too strong for that. Mind you, they were the days when such words as 'pregnant' were banned from the media.

Sophistication is what we aspired to achieve. That meant admiring homes with flat roofs. It meant asking for capuccino (and saying *grazie*) in the new espresso bars. It meant

11

buying rye bread in preference to vienna. It meant having a girlfriend who wore black stockings (a pox on Panti-hose for making obsolete that marvellous piece of warm leg twixt stocking-top and panties). It meant pretending not to be uneasy in the company of homosexuals.

As I remember, beer was non-u so we drank claret or vermouth and coke. And we frequented the Savoy Theatre, the Omonia Restaurant, the Balaika Wine Bar and the Eltham art colony. And the most desirable girlfriends patterned themselves on Juliette Greco or Sally Bowles. Of course, we lived in a world without jets or TV sets, feeling ourselves trapped in a rank, cultural backwater or billabong. So we put art on a pedestal, reading novels by the score, all but living in second-hand bookshops.

Included on our list of essential reading were Carson McCullers, Ralph Ellison and, of course, J D Salinger, whose Holden Caulfield was to be the precursor of so many confused, inarticulate adolescents. Dustin Hoffman's Graduate for one. But no wonder they're inarticulate. Shortly thereafter the young abandoned the novel.

The Fifties. The Korean War was winding down and Mao was declaring his intention of letting those hundred flowers bloom. The French were facing defeat at Dien Bien Phu, Fidel Castro was planning the overthrow of Batista, Krushchev was preparing his denunciation of Stalin and Stanley Kramer came to Melbourne to film *On The Beach*.

Apart from some desultory protests against nuclear tests, my friends couldn't have cared less about politics. Given Menzies' total dominance of Canberra and Australia's obedience to British dictates, it seemed an area that was best forgotten. Instead they listened to the Goon Show on radio or visited the New Theatre to see a young comedian called Barry Humphries. And with necessity the mother of invention they furnished their flats with inexpensive Victoriana and tried using hessian for wallpaper and curtains. And they allowed themselves the odd American film, providing it starred Marlon Brando or James Dean. Or they listened to Indian music or Leadbelly at all-hours parties. Or they went off to see *Look Back in Anger* at the Union Theatre, going to Luna Park on the way home.

Soon television got under way and many people I knew joined the channels, full of ideas and idealism. The medium was destined to awaken the dormant intellect of our nation. It would educate and inspire.

Whereas in the past any has-been American entertainer could make a fortune at Stadium concerts, television would interpret Australians for themselves and the world, freeing us from the cultural cringe. It was just another example of our certainty, of the confidence we felt. Without doubt, we were going to be the agents of profound social change.

The Fifties were times for talking, for endless, egocentric discussions. It was a time for writing short stories and for flamboyant behaviour, for emotional intensity, for eloquence, for falling in love.

Now it seems that most of that has gone, to be replaced by coolness, introspection and, in the wake of Vietnam, by a numbness and inertia. Increasingly the young are incommunicative, even among themselves, and our élitist notions of excellence, of art on a pedestal, have been replaced by a tolerance that smacks of hopelessness and what-the-hell.

In a book of short stories, John Updike described an exodus of young people. They leave their homes and climb a rocky hill overlooking a Massachusetts township. There they sit, silent and inert, looking down on their city and their folks. Their presence and their passivity slowly unnerves the citizenry who draw their blinds and shutter their windows. Updike's story ends with these words.

The town seems to be tightening like a fist, a glistening clot of apoplectic signs and sun-struck, stalled automobiles. And the Hillies were slowly withdrawing upward. They were getting ready for our attack.

Could that be the difference? The difference between the young of the Fifties and the young of today? It is simply that we thought we were going to win, to triumph, whereas the young now feel overwhelmed and doomed? Has our smug self-importance been replaced by their self-pity? There are certainly elements of despair in their music, in their movies, suggesting that romanticism has been overwhelmed by fatalism.

The Renaissance was a movement that, in the first instance, involved only a handful of people. But that ultimately changed the world by setting new standards in writing, painting and architecture. Currently, we see the antithesis of renaissance, as vast numbers capitulate entirely to pop culture, embracing the low-browed and the instantly accessible instead of the complex and aspiring. It's as if their motto was 'if it's not worth doing, it's not worth doing well' and they were applying that motto to life itself.

The social consensus seems to be that the young of today are lucky that they're given it all on a plate. But I'm not so sure. It seems to me they've good cause for their weariness, given the growing ghastliness of urban life. Thinking back, it was better in the Fifties when the young were just beginning to assert themselves. Because beginnings are always more optimistic.

Time held me green and dying
Though I sang in my chains like the sea.

Dylan Thomas

Cinderella
and other tales
of subversion

My dear Prime Minister,

I have, as you requested, investigated the various nursery rhymes and fairy stories being told in Australia's kindergartens and schools. As a result, it is my duty to inform you that ASIO's allegations are substantially correct, that many of the stories are of foreign origin and express quite unacceptable political or moral views.

Let us consider the case of *Cinderella*, which tells of a working-class girl who aspires to marry a handsome prince. Clearly this is capable of a number of differing interpretations.

On the one hand, Cinderella has a strong ambition to improve her social standing, something that we much admire in Liberal circles. Unfortunately, her means of achieving this ambition is through intervention of a more powerful force, viz., a fairy godmother. And as you are aware, during the brief and catastrophic Labor Government, there was a tendency to use various Ministers as fairy godmothers who distributed largesse from the Treasury.

So it seems to me that Cinderella's dreams are fulfilled, as it were, by a sort of Federal grant which is inconsistent with the political realities at this point in time whilst being in direct conflict with your own philosophies. After all, working people are being asked to lower their expectancies. So either we'll have to rewrite the story so that Cinderella obtains her coach and gold slippers through (a) an increase in productivity and (b) frugal living, or we'll need to delete it from the approved text.

Or you might prefer us to provide schools with a revised version in which Cinderella stays happily in her hearth, knowing her place. She could be reminded that, at her salary level, she'll enjoy the full rate of indexation and that public ward care will be available under Medibank should her consumption of soot and dust cause health problems.

This brings me to *The Tortoise and the Hare,* a story that's totally opposed to the theories of Ayn Rand. We have entrepreneurial capitalism, as embodied in the hare, losing the race to the inch-by-inch progress of the tortoise. Clearly this race result would be a blow to business confidence. On the other hand, we could tell children the tortoise represents the good, solid worker who, instead of insisting on fat salary rises and speedy improvement in working conditions, patiently slogs away and is all the better for it in the long run.

But given the ambiguity of the images, we feel it would be safer to eliminate this story altogether.

On the other hand, *Sleeping Beauty* poses no problems whatsoever. All that is needed are some minor alterations to the illustrations accompanying the story so that the correct conclusions are drawn.

We see the sleeping princess wearing a sash carrying the slogan: 'Australian industry in the doldrums'. We see the forest of nettles labelled 'Labor policies'. And we see the handsome prince who slashes away with upraised sword and puckered lips as being identified with your good self. In this way the child will see industry revived by the mouth-to-mouth resuscitation of your splendid Government.

Some members of the committee were troubled by *Little Red Riding Hood,* not simply because of the unfortunate colour of her garment (this matter needs also to be raised in reference to *The Little Red Hen*) but because of possible interpretations.

Some respondents in our research programme readily identified Ms Hood with the city, while the hungry wolf was seen as symbolising the rapacity of Australian farmers. The little basket carried by the child was suspected to contain unemployment benefits and superphosphate bounties. Once again, we recommend that the story be withdrawn from general usage as infants are extremely impressionable.

In contrast, *The Little Red Hen,* is an excellent piece of propaganda for the rural industry. The splendid fowl sets about planting, raising and harvesting grain without any help from the uncaring populace. Indeed, they deride her efforts. Yet when the grain has been made into wheat and hence into life-sustaining loaves of bread, everyone rushes to eat it. What a perfect expression of the situation in this country where the urban populations are totally disinterested in the problems of the farmer. Moreover, the moral of the story, which has the hen (not red, I submit) eating bread alone, should bring home to the city electorates a sense of their ultimate dependency on their country cousins.

There are a number of stories which deal effectively with the dole-bludger. Take *The Grasshopper and the Ant.* In this account the ants represent the stable, well-behaved workforce striving constantly for the ultimate good of the entire community. No go-slows or stop-work meetings. No one works to regulations or goes on strike.

In contrast, there's a large grasshopper who exhibits dropout tendencies, clearly preferring singing and dancing to working. Unfortunately the ants take pity on this worthless creature and, unlike the more conservative hen, evince socialist tendencies by allowing him to share their food.

I'm in favour of the story remaining in the repertoire, as it were, provided the grasshopper freezes to death in the snow. Incidentally, one committee member has suggested that we update the story by having the grasshopper a member of a rock group or at very least electrifying his fiddle.

I think that both *Goldilocks and the Three Bears* and *Snow White and the Seven Dwarfs* can be eliminated on moral grounds. It's bad enough having a peroxide-blonde nymphette sleeping in bears' beds, without having a girl of excellent character cohabiting with seven dwarfs. Clearly these are quite unsuitable for Australian children.

But then, we suspect that some of these stories were written by one Hans Andersen, who whilst claiming to be Christian, comes from those Scandinavian countries where permissiveness and perversion are rampant.

Jack and the Beanstalk presents a number of problems. On the one hand, it emphasises the plight of the rural sector which your coalition partners will enthusiastically endorse. In particular, the sale of a cow for a few worthless beans emphasises the plight of the beef industry. However, this may tend to intensify the political protest from both the beef and dairy people. Worse still, the beanstalk could be seen as thriving on the superphosphate bounty while the giant could be viewed as big government. As you know, many ill-informed critics suggest that the farmers are stealing a great many golden eggs from Treasury. All in all, on balance, all things considered, we favour the tale's elimination.

We recommend a few subtle changes to *Hansel and Gretel,* both in regard to the text and its interpretive illustrations.

We see Hansel and Gretel as the innocent electorate being lured into the forest by the blandishments of the ALP. What better symbol for the ALP's election promises than a gingerbread cottage? Once inside this seductive building, they find they're to be devoured by the very person who promised them succour.

Having read this amended version to schoolchildren, we found that they went and hid their faces when exposed to a photograph of Margaret Whitlam.

18

Next story on our list is *The Emperor's New Clothes.* Unfortunately, the rather fatuous central character in his imaginary regalia reminds radical elements of Sir John Kerr. Clearly we've enough demonstrations against the monarchy's representative already.

For years mothers have been telling children the story of *The Ugly Duckling* without realising that it is a seditious Bolshevik fable. Once again, as in *Cinderella,* the downtrodden in society are told to expect a miraculous reversion of their fortunes. Clearly this hints at the urgent need for revolution, so that *all* the ugly ducklings can become swans. We believe that this story should be banned immediately and charges laid against any subversive who attempts to tell it.

In contrast, the committee found *The Three Little Pigs* to be a solid bourgeois morality tale with special appeal to middle-class home owners and to the small shopkeeper. As well, the major companies involved in brickbuilding can only applaud its general tenor.

In essence, the story tells how two decent, solid citizens build their own homes only to have them blown down by the dark, wolf-like forces of radicalism. Whereupon these completely respectable taxpayers are devoured. However, the third pig prepares for the worst by building in brick and is able to both ward off and ultimately destroy the enemy of society. Clearly here is a parable about the individual in society, about self-help and about ideological purity.

Alternatively, the story has the potential to help our Defence Minister, but in this case the first two pigs would have to be seen as countries ill-prepared to defend themselves from an outside threat — whereas the third pig, like Australia currently, is preparing to fight off any huffing and puffing from Marxism's expansionist forces.

This brings us to the nursery rhymes which, as you know, almost invariably began their lives as political tracts. Therefore it is proper to view them in political terms today.

Thus we view the sad story of *Humpty Dumpty* as a warning to those who would oppose orderly egg marketing. The various egg boards around Australia are constantly faced with the problems of farmers who sell their goods outside the system, sometimes smuggling them interstate. This could lead to the fragile balance in the industry being disturbed, with the result that all the 'king's men' in the marketing bureaucracies would be unable to remedy the situation.

More positive imagery is provided by the rhyme which has a cow jumping over the Moon: given the dispirited state of the dairy industry, this exhilarating image might have a very therapeutic effect.

It's much the same with *Baa Baa Black Sheep* and *This Little Pig Went to Market* which, respectively, suggest a rosy future for our woolgrowers and our pig men.

We disapprove of *Wee Willie Winkie* on moral grounds as anyone who rushes around the city in his nightgown is suspect. Furthermore Mr Winkie seems to spread his favours both upstairs and downstairs, showing a lamentable lack of class consciousness.

Nor should *Ten Little Nigger Boys* be encouraged as its ever-diminishing number of blacks reminded some of our respondents of certain unfortunate occurrences in Tasmania, not to mention the infant mortality rate among Aborigines on mission stations.

As for *Jack be Nimble, Jack be Quick,* some group members identified that rhyme with Sir John Egerton's acceptance of a knighthood — with many of the more Left-leaning interviewees making uncouth suggestions as to what might be done with the candle.

Yours sincerely,

Professor Basil Goodbody
(University of Queensland)

Why nations
go to pot

While the rest of the Press is obsessed with the meaningless miscellanea men call news, I choose to write about such epic and eternal issues as love, life and death. And today is no exception. I propose revealing, for the first time, the real reason for the ectopia in our imbroglioed personal lives and socio-political relationships. Some blame bomb tests or fornication or faithlessness for the chaos that engulfs us, stretching our nerves like the E-string on Segovia's guitar while crumbling the foundations of our noble institutions. But while it's obvious to any fool that the current spate of earthquakes was provoked by the change to decimal currency, the root cause for the spread of anarchy and despair lies elsewhere – in the decline of tea-drinking in Western society.

I detest the way some people make sweeping generalisations about blacks, Italians, homosexuals. At the same time, I must say that anyone who doesn't drink gallons of tea tends to be untrustworthy, disloyal, mean, greedy and generally worthless. It's probably the one thing that Richard Nixon had in common with Hitler, Rameses I and Atilla the Hun.

Tea, thou soft, thou sober and venerable liquid. Tea, the very elixir of civilisation and the nectar of the angels. Tea, from the people who brought us the dim-sim, the penny bunger and the archaeological exhibition. For the fragrant leaves were discovered by a Chinese chappy in 2700 BC, thus ensuring Peking's historical pre-eminence. Indeed, the word has become central to oriental philosophy, meaning virtue, cleanliness and noble aspiration.

Consider the fact that Britain didn't really earn the adjective 'Great' until tea became popular in the early part of the 18th century. Indeed, many argue that it wasn't until the Duke and Duchess of Bedford invented afternoon tea in 1840 that Britain began to fulfil its national and imperial destiny. Macauley's description of a friend could be the portrait of Britain at its most buoyant and bullish: 'Blinking, puffing, rolling his head, tearing his meat like a tiger and swallowing his tea in oceans.'

And talk of tea and oceans recalls the birth of the United States of America. You'll remember that the infamous Tea Act provoked some Bostonians to tip a few tons of Bushells into their harbour in 1773. As a result, the Gulf Stream carried it right around the coast and as the tea-stained waves beat upon the shores, the colonies became nations.

Tea, though an oriental
Is a gentleman at least
Cocoa is a cad and coward
Cocoa is a vulgar beast.

When Chesterton wrote those words the sentiments were admirable. But he got his beans confused. For what happened when America switched its allegiance to coffee? The Depression, McCarthyism and Watergate. It's the same in the UK, where you can't get a decent cup for love or money. Britain went to pot as soon as it left the pot for the percolator and the espresso machine, those contemptible pieces of plumbing that have long since debilitated your Greeks, Turks and Italians. (And what an ungrateful mob the Poms really are. Without the kettle [for tea] inspiring James Watt the Industrial Revolution wouldn't have happened.)

Is it any wonder that ninety per cent of Americans are heroin addicts when they've never known the transcendental joy of a good cuppa? When the nearest they've come to its ambrosial delights is via those twin blasphemies, instant tea and the tea-bag? As the Japanese have known for a thousand years, tea isn't merely a drink. It is a religion, a sacrament, requiring graceful ceremony. So whether you're a geisha or a swaggy you'll have your ritualistic way of suffusing the fragrant and sacred leaves. So that 'instant' and 'tea' are not simply contradiction in terms; they are anathema. As for the tea-bag, lolling in the cup like a drowned rat, that was invented by one of the most contemptible traitors in history. I refer to Thomas Sullivan, tea dealer of New York, who used to offer samples in little bags of silk. May he jiggle in hell for his perfidy.

Jiggling. The word is jangling and crass, echoing the incessant rhythm of the percolator, which, in turn, reminds one of the Latin-American beat of Brazil, the country that grows those accursed beans. When I read, just last week, that Brazil's coffee crop had failed, putting the entire national economy at risk, my cup ranneth over. Jiggling bags indeed. Tea means leaves. Leaves for stirring, for straining, for reading in the empty cup. Leaves for poking down the kitchen sink with your finger or putting on the maidenhair. Tea without leaves is a negation of the whole idea – like sex without gender or having a shower in your overcoat.

Not that I'm snobbish about tea. Not for me your Earl Grey in its crested, Royal Appointment tins from Fortnum and Mason. Though I do have a soft spot for Twining's Irish Workingman's Tea, I'll stick with Bushells and Griffiths in their little paper packets that spill everywhere when you open them and always conceal a spoonful in their innermost folds, even when you've shaken them into your battered tin and buried the spoon. For me, tea is essentially democratic and tastes best of all after prolonged stewing, when served in thick railway cups.

And none of your 'one for each person and one for the pot'. Make it three each and two for luck, so that the spoon dissolves during stirring. Tea should be indistinguishable from Marveer in taste, colour and its effect on furniture. And it should be drunk while still boiling, so that the oesphagus knows what's hit it. Either that, or it should be enjoyed in enamel mugs, Fred McCubbin-style, under a gum tree whose leaves have been added to the billy.

Now there's a thought. We're a nation of cultural cringers who tug our forelocks at French cooking while bemoaning our lack of indigenous dishes. Yet how many restaurants are willing to serve billy tea? How many head waiters know how to swing one over their head? Ask them to try and they'd say it was too dangerous, that it could splash a few droplets on the chandelier. Yet they think nothing of the risks of those dishes flambé beloved of American tourists and successful used-car salesmen. In most Australian restaurants they ignite half the things on the menu, from soup to soufflé.

This nation was built on a cup of tea, a Bex, and a good lie-down. Realising that Australia's decline dates from the rise of Nescafé and the introduction of tea bags, remain a patriot. Or perhaps, a potriot. While refusing to budge for the national anthem or *Advance Australia Fair,* I rise to my feet, eyes brimming, when the band plays *I'm a Little Teapot Short and Stout.* And I cannot hear that old Bushells jingle, 'In every home, in every place, wherever you may be, it always will be welcome, that cup of Bushells tea' without a soulful sob.

Moreover, I intend to go to a grave marked by the following words by Samuel Johnson.

He was a hardened and shameless tea drinker, who for twenty years diluted his meals with only the infusion of that fascinating plant, whose kettle had scarcely time to cool: who with tea amused the evening, with tea solaced the midnight and with tea welcomed the morn.

Not for me RIP. I'd prefer RIT; rather than being buried or burned, I'd like to be pickled in a brew of Bushells. Or else, in honour of tea's Chinese origins, to be laid out like the jade princess in a suit made from all those green Lan-Choo labels my Mum's been saving since 1942.

I'm told that a cup of tea contains just four calories, while being rich in B-complex vitamins, tannin, nicotinic acid, caffeine and volatile oils. But the chemists have yet to isolate the magic ingredient responsible for tea's special alchemy, its ability to lift the spirits and block the sink.

The rich are bleeding: ask my chauffeur

As you know, I am the President of the Rich Persons' Society with branches in Toorak and Darling Point. And while very tolerant on questions of race and creed (we'll accept almost any suitable white Protestant) we *are* rather sensitive on the question of class.

Subsequently, as the name of our society implies, membership is only available to persons who are rich: either fairly, very or filthy. We rich are beginning to feel like a beleaguered species, along with the kangaroo, the blue whale and the Uruguayan aardvark. Yet while people protest the extermination of these worthy creatures, one hears few voices raised in our defence. Those who endanger us are never boycotted, blacklisted or greenbanned. No one gathers petitions in our favour.

Yet in rapid succession we've witnessed the French Revolution, the Russian Revolution and the election of Whitlam's yobbo Government. Clearly such unpalatable events are gaining momentum which makes it all the more important for rich persons to close ranks and protect their status.

Today I wish to address members of the Rich Persons' Society on the vexed question of inflation. For while our fortunes are protected by capital gains, our incomes have been eroded by this unpleasant phenomenon. So here are some suggestions on how rich persons can slow the progress of this economic canker, while at the same time conserving the loot that sets us apart from the malodorous plebeians.

To make this interesting, let's take a typical day.

You awake in the morning and go to the bathroom, where you are saving money by: (a) Turning off the electric seat warmer; and (b) Refusing to buy toilet tissue.

Instead, you've hung half a dozen copies of the *Illustrated London News* from a nail or, alternatively, you've put your old copies of *Who's Who* in the loo. Apart from being terribly kitsch and amusing, this will save you approximately $12 per year. Then you go downstairs to the diningroom, where you turn a blind eye to the unstarched napkins and have a spartan breakfast of bread and dripping. Flown in especially from Fortnum and Mason, the dripping is quite exquisite at just $45 a 4-oz. tin.

It is now around 10.30 and time for the office. However, you do not take the Bentley. Instead, you take the Jaguar, reminding the grumbling chauffeur that until the Liberals are safely back in power it will be necessary to rough it.

Arriving at the office, you refuse any staff requests for an increase and, to lower overheads, fire a few senior executives who've been with you for thirty years. Needless to say, both the golden handshake and the gold watch are out of the question in the present economic climate and should be replaced by a firm handshake and some encouraging words. It is, after all, the thought that counts.

This will take you to 12.00 and time for lunch. Remember it is most important to eat something, even if it is just four or five courses. We do not advocate skipping a midday meal, given the importance of post-meridian decision-making. Once ensconced at the table, you should make every effort to cut back your lunch from four hours to three or even less. This can be achieved by cutting back to half a dozen oysters and by skipping the chocolate mousse and your cigar and port. However, remember that sudden shock of a three-

27

hour lunch can cause unpleasant side effects such as hunger pangs and weight loss.

But the most effective way of fighting inflation in the restaurant is to curtail the practice of tipping. After all, your waiter probably voted Labor and so has only himself to blame. In any case, he will realise that at a time of crisis we must all pull in our belts.

Arriving back at the office at say, 3.15, it is important to work in a leisurely manner. Apart from being weakened by your inadequate diet, any vigorous activity may further heat an already over-heated economy. So simply sit back and doodle on your blotter with your gold Parker. Alternatively, you might take the time to console your secretary whose request for a salary raise you're forced to refuse in a firm but kindly manner. (Take the poor lass upon your knee and explain both the stock market slump and latest OEDC figures.)

Meanwhile, your wife will be busy with her charity work. In the past she's often spent $500 on a dress and $50 on a hair-do prior to raising $40 for some worthy cause like the Lord Mayor's Leprosy Fund. Now she's realised that charity begins in the mansion, and she spent the afternoon accordingly. (Here the trick is to be vague about the purpose of donations and not to issue receipts.)

Towards evening your wife will be supervising cook. Here some ruthless measures will be necessary. For example, it has been your custom to slop the Seaview Cabernet Sauvignon '68 in the cooking. Well, some members of the Rich Persons' Society are now making do with Seaview Cabernet '72. Apart from anything else, this will impress the staff with your determination and recall the spirit of Dunkirk.

On leaving the office, your chauffeur will be sulking at the wheel of the Jaguar, ashamed at being seen in such a low-grade hack. Now is the time to warn him you're considering travelling by public transport. Tell him you have already inquired about purchasing a bus or tram.

On arriving home, you open the door yourself and settle back and enjoy the few nips of Black Label in a chipped enamel mug. You then put on some favourite music, taking care to play your stereophonic records monaurally. It's in these subtle ways that we can turn the inflationary tide. You'll remember that you opened your front door yourself. This is because the butler has been out begging all afternoon, having been issued with a pair of dark glasses, a white stick and another chipped enamel mug. (Granted, this involves a small capital outlay, but the return can be excellent.)

While counting the take, you remind the family retainer that he's to take the empty Dom Perignon bottles back to the licensed grocer and demand a deposit. Should he show any signs of resentment at his new duties, simply remind him of the horrifying conditions in the workhouse.

While on the subject of servants, remember to turn off the second bar on their Vulcan Conray. And remember to feed them on Luv dog food, which is rich in protein. When spread on thin slices of dry toast, they won't be able to pick it from *paté*.

Remember, too, that you should keep your staff as well fed as possible. After all, if the situation worsens they may be required to make the supreme sacrifice. The Rich Persons' Society will shortly be publishing a recipe book, *A Hundred Delicious Ways to Serve the Servants*.

These are dark and difficult days. Yet we're not alone in our suffering. The patron of the Rich Persons' Society, Her Majesty the Queen, is also suffering under a Labour Government and is setting us a wonderful example. Consider that she's no longer changing the guard at Buckingham Palace, thus saving a fortune on Nappy Wash.

The flag-fall gladiators

Consider democracy's chauffeur, the taxi driver. Not for him the faithfulness of the family retainer, burnishing his master's Bentley. Completely promiscuous, he'll go anywhere, anytime, with anyone, with a loud whistle and change in his pocket. Flaunting the garish colours of the trollop, reeking of the cheap scent of the car deodoriser (in the plastic flower quivering atop a rubber suction cap) he's forever on the prowl, on the beat. Carnal cars, with leering *VACANT* signs.

Yet the taxi driver is not without his heroism. Yellow, Silver Top and RSL may lack the military discipline of the First Hussars or the Light Brigade, yet at the fall of their flags they hurl themselves into the valleys and the freeways and the intersections of death. Horns blazing, they charge

30

the red lights and ask no quarter. Dangers to the left of them, peril to the right of them, with their faith pinned in a plated medal of Christopher, that deregistered saint.

You are all familiar with the careless courage of the Australian taxi driver. You hear his stream of abuse in every stream of traffic. Yet his fearlessness pales into inconsequence beside the gay abandon of the Parisian who hurls his battered Citroen into the cacophonic fray with the brave fatalism of an Edith Piaf lyric. *C'est la vie, c'est la mort.*

Le Mans is an anti-climax after the boulevards of Paris, after you circle the great squares and the fountains with a centrifugal force beyond the wildest dreams of Luna Park. But the silent screams of the tourists in the back seats are a stifled yawn beside the blind terror of a Roman taxi, where the driver is either a frustrated Fangio or a deranged communist who accelerates in tempo to his diatribe against the Church and the *fascisti.*

The only time I've ever been close to converting to Catholicism was in a Fiat taxi as it hurtled through the back alleys and Vespas en route to the Vatican. Perhaps it's an arrangement they have made for the cab companies. Certainly you're delivered to St. Peter's Square in a frame of mind to throw yourself before the altar or to make a lavish donation in your gratitude for surviving.

But even the Romans aren't the worst. They come a bad second to the Japanese. Talk about *Death Race 2000.* First of all, the Japanese driver refuses to leave his seat, opening the side door by yanking at a Heath Robinson lever. Nor is it any good asking for access to the boot as that is completely occupied by giant lp gas tanks. This anti-pollution measure seems totally unnecessary as I'm quite sure that if Japanese cars were fitted with appropriate carburettors they could be powered by the fumes in the air. Then you're off on the downtown run, behind a young man totally committed to the spirit of kamikaze. There's scarcely any need for street lighting, given the burning wrecks at every crossing.

31

And if Japan has achieved ZPG it's not through contraception or abortion. It's a consequence of the mayhem that occurs when taxis take swerving short cuts through narrow, crowded lanes. The only time I've been close to converting to Shinto . . .

Moscow is very different. Like elections, taxis are few and far between. For all the official disapproval of capitalism, the Russian taxi is a grotesque parody of Detroit design, circa 1945, although on a less extravagant scale. Thus most of the room in a Russian taxi is taken up by the driver who invariably seems to have sought political asylum having fled the cast of World Championship Wrestling. Such is their breadth of shoulder that they fully occupy the front seat, thus obliterating much of the view.

As well, the Russian driver is profoundly silent, with an occasional *da, nyet,* or grunt being the best you can expect from even a comparative chatterbox. And there's a very odd thing about the Moscovite cabby – in fact, about all their drivers. Which is that they hide their windscreen wipers. They take them off, wrap them up and lock them in their boot. Then, at the first sign of rain, all the cars stop while everyone gets out and reverses the procedure. I was never able to find out why, but I suspect that people pinch them, that the only windscreen wiper company in all the Russias, presumably located in Omsk, has had trouble with its five-year plan.

However, there's one aspect of the Russian taxi service that is wholly admirable. You've only to mention the need for a taxi in your hotel room for it to chug up to the front steps. Presumably the KGB officials monitoring your conversations on the ill-concealed microphones pass on the bookings.

English taxis are, of course, unique. Instead of being long and awkward, they're built with the vertical emphasis, like a policeman's helmet. The interiors have seats all around plus a little switch for a radiator, so that it's a little like being

32

driven around in a bed-sitter. And such is the driver's knowledge of their ancient city that they can take hours to travel a few blocks, having driven furiously all the time. Thus the uninitiated get the impression that Soho, for example, is approximately the size of Los Angeles. As well as this artful dodging, this determination to take the most circuitous route so as to maximise income, the typical driver combines a spurious deference with a killer's instinct. Not even the cabbies of New York can be as vicious if a tip is considered inadequate. 'If I ever see you again', I recall one snarling on my first trip to London, 'I'll effing well run over you'.

As it happens, New York's taxi drivers are changing their character. The old style hack, looking like Jimmy Cagney or Archie Bunker, is on the way out. If you believe them, that's because of all the muggings. Yet while every cabby I've ever talked to carries a spanner at the ready, and has stories galore of bashings and heists, only one had had direct experience. 'I've just got outa hospital. Some black punks mugged me,' he drawled around a mouthful of soggy, extinct cigar. 'All they got was $10 and I got four months in bed. I'm getting out at the end of this year. Moving in with the son and daughter-in-law in Queens.'

Curiously these stories of violence and danger are told with pride, with a sort of inverse patriotism. It's like listening to returned soldiers reminiscing on old campaigns. Such is the New Yorker's xenophobia, his brutalised camaraderie, that he regards the outsider with contempt, a civvy.

The new taxi drivers of New York still throw their great saffron tanks around with the same aggression and skill. You see them surging through the crowds of steam that rise from New York's underworld, muscling their way through the most battered traffic on earth. For here the driving style is king-sized dodgem and it's hard to see a car in Manhattan that doesn't cry out for panel beating. Yet I suspect that motorists wear these scars proudly as further evidence of what it's like to live in a battlefield.

The difference with the new drivers is that they're twenty, thirty years younger and much cooler. They loll back in the seat and twirl the power steering with one finger. And they talk to you through the grille, about America's fascism in South America, about the murder of Allende, about corruption in every level of politics. And they'll turn out to be a disenchanted computer programmer from IBM or an erstwhile member of an executive training scheme. Unlike the older men, these drop-out drivers are quite happy to accept a fare to an area like Brooklyn. Less interested in exaggerating the dangers in New York, they're concerned with the bigger picture, with the goings-on in the White House and the Pentagon.

As a bloke in a Yellow cab said to me yesterday, on the way from Mascot: 'Taxi driving is the last form of pure capitalism. We don't get any holiday pay. We don't get workers' comp. unless we insure ourselves. Trade unions can't get to first base with taxi drivers. We're too independent, too competitive.' It's an odd profession which includes everyone from the Greek owner-drivers who bought a plate in preference to a fish shop, to under-employed actors who learn their Hector Crawford scripts whilst waiting in the theatre rank. I've had a driver who was the worst sort of white Australia racist, who spent the entire trip talking of his hatred of wogs, of how he'd refuse to pick them up if they were the last fare on Earth, or of how he'd deliberately drop them off at the wrong destination.

And I remember his astonishment when it dawned on him that I didn't share his prejudices. Then there was the ardent supporter of the PLO who was still fighting and re-fighting the Six-Day War that cost him his Palestine home. I've met drivers who've chosen the profession because they like to talk to people and to set their own pace – and others who grate their gears and their teeth because they hate their cars, their job and their passengers, seeing every red light as a personal insult.

34

I've had sign-language fights with Mexican drivers who pretended their meters were broken and have sat two hours in a motionless traffic jam in Rio de Janeiro with a meter that had a Latin American tick. I've been driven through the night of Warsaw by a driver intent on giving me black market zlotys for my precious American dollars. And I have been abused for my whiteness by a black power zealot on my way to see the fabled Watts Towers in a ghetto of Los Angeles. But undoubtedly my most memorable experience in a taxi was in Prague, arguably the most beautiful city in all of eastern Europe.

Having been there just after the Russian invasion, I returned on the anniversary of Palach's suicide to find the city all but closed down with guards carrying machine guns patrolling Wenceslas Square where the buildings were still pock marked with Russian gun fire. The street lights keep going out – sabotage at the power works. The local Stalinists had been busy painting out the pro-Dubcek slogans but had been too dim-witted to remove the images of the good soldier Schweik, the most enduring and lovable embodiment of the Czech spirit.

We'd spent a tragic day talking to friends in the film industry, most of whom had been purged from their jobs in favour of hard-line-toeing mediocrities. Feeling very melancholy, we were walking through the Charles University, the oldest in Europe, which had been closed down on a pretext (a fictitious flu epidemic) lest the students attempt to demonstrate in Palach's memory. Whereupon a Skoda taxi came bounding over the cobbles and we hailed it. To our surprise and pleasure, the driver spoke in good, though slightly accented English. He was a striking man in his forties and in a remarkably unguarded conversation, we learnt that he knew many of our friends, including the charming Czechoslovakian woman who'd translated Alan Marshall's *I Can Jump Puddles*.

He could also explain what had happened to some of the

faces we'd missed when visiting publishers or the film school. It seemed that this cameraman was now working as an office cleaner, while this director had been luckier, escaping to America where he was teaching at UCLA. As for so-and-so, she was now washing dishes, just as Dubcek was rumoured to be cutting firewood in the north.

'As for myself, I was a member of the faculty at Charles University until they sacked me a few months ago. Now I drive a taxi. And I consider myself very lucky to have such a good job. Because I can get around a bit and talk to people. Please, tell Australia about the situation here. Tell them that in Prague, the taxis are driven by professors of history.' And I still remember his roar of laughter, at once ironic, angry and triumphant.

The
joyous contraption

Like Toad in *The Wind In The Willows,* I like cars. I know
that I shouldn't; that today's showroom fantasy is tomorrow's
rusting hulk; that they're air-polluting, city-choking,
resource-consuming, money-wasting, ego-boosting and anti-
social. Yet still, for all that, I find them the most joyous
of contraptions. And that goes equally for the Rolls-Royce
with its gothic grille or for those little Japanese cars that
look like motorised dim-sims.

Manufacturers are forever giving their cars aggressively
masculine names like Hunter, Rapier, Jaguar, Rover and

Charger. Yet the car is essentially a female thing, a sex object for the male chauvinist. Thus Holden is to be congratulated for calling one model the Monaro, which is, I'm told, Aboriginal for a woman's breast. *Exactly* right. Consider the mammiferous surge of the mudguards, the voluptuous curve of the buttock-like boot. A car is a fickle, temperamental, teasing, exciting and expensive creature, a ducoed Bardot. Yet the only vehicles that are christened with women's names are the giant semis – the truckies paint *Debbie* or *Julie* on the bonnets. And a big truck has all the femininity and allure of a Turkish wrestler.

At the last census, I'd owned twenty cars. The first was a little green Austin of rather bulbous design that I bought from a used car dealer at Essendon. I'd never driven in my life, but managed to bunny-hop it to the city where I immediately applied for a licence. The dealer had given me the name of a co-operative constable at the back of the Exhibition Building who, in return for a counter lunch, would turn a blind eye to such minor matters as signalless turns, kerb-hitting and a total ignorance of the road law.

It served me well, that Austin. I soon developed a feeling of invincibility, a ringing conviction that car accidents were something that happened to statistics and that road laws, like most of the Ten Commandments, could happily be ignored. This is a view shared by most young motorists, one that comes to grief with one's first accident. As it happens, it wasn't my fault on that particular occasion, but as I'd deserved to crash on one hundred other occasions, I'd little basis for complaint.

Suddenly my little car was scattered across an intersection. I have a memory of lots of green shards, like lawn clippings. There was nothing large enough for the tow truck to get its hook into. So while they took me off to the hospital (the *Austin* Hospital) for panel beating, the last remains of my faithful droshky were being swept up for scattering on some smoking tip.

Then came my Goggomobile. This was even smaller than the Austin, approximately the size of a hip bath. I'd seen a photo of a Goggo in the paper, being driven around Knightsbridge by one of Princess Margaret's eligible bachelors. And it was love at first squint. I think it appealed to the little boy in me, by recalling the happy days spent pushing Dinkys around in the dust at East Kew Primary. At the same time, it seemed the quintessence of sophistication to have a car so small it would fit in its own boot. Well, if the Honorable Barrington Twickenham-Fynne took Princess Margaret to Ascot in a Goggo, it would have to be just the thing for taking one's girl friend to the drive-in.

I remember being somewhat deflated as I made my maiden voyage from the showroom. 'Look Mummy,' said a brat on the footpath, 'Noddy's car!' And it didn't work out too well at the drive-in, either. For a start they wouldn't let me in unless it was a General Exhibition picture and even then the speaker cable wasn't long enough and we couldn't see over the car in front. And finally, there simply wasn't space for two people, a couple of bottles of Passiona, a bag of chips and a hamburger. Let alone for any funny business.

The Goggo turned out to be more like a corset than a car. Worse still, being two stroke, it was as hard to start as a lawn mower and brought out the killer in other, larger vehicles. Suddenly, normally peace-loving family sedans would lunge at you with carnivorous leers on their grilles. I could have coped with all that, but the damned thing kept breaking down. And, being so small, it was no good going to a mechanic. You had to take it to the jewellers.

I well remember the Goggo lying doggo when I was doing some filming with Bobby Limb, then at the height of his TV career. Poor Bob, he had to push me all the way through a crowded Kew Junction, shouting epithets quite inconsistent with his family image. It marked the beginning of his ratings slump. Finally, I had another spectacular collision which reduced the fibreglass body to a shower of glistening filaments. Whereupon I bought a Beetle.

They call the VW Hitler's car. Well, mine really *was* Hitler's car. Because of bullet holes in the muffler, the engine roared like a Nuremberg rally, while the car showed anti-Semitic tendencies at pedestrian crossings. But such was its mechanical reliability that despite the creaks and groans that you'd expect from a war veteran, it *never* stopped running. Not even when you turned off the ignition. It would sit in the garage coughing and farting for ages. About the only way you *could* stop it was by syphoning out the petrol, something the car clearly recalled from its black-market days in Berlin. Thus my third wreck, from the Third Reich, was sold to a thorough-going Nazi at a used car yard and replaced by a succession of vehicles that have grown dim in the memory. They included a Peugeot (the French Holden), a Karmann Ghia (the homosexual version of the Volkswagen) and my pride and joy, a 2.4 Jaguar.

I remember when I went into Brysons to buy the thing. For all my penchant for gleaming cars, I was and remain, extremely shabby in personal appearance. So I presented myself in their chandeliered showroom in a somewhat perished pair of rubber thongs, some corduroy trousers stiffened with paint and a beard looking like last year's bird's nest. Much to my annoyance, the salesman peered superciliously at me through his glass partition before returning to his newspaper. Impatiently, I cleared my throat in what I hoped was an appropriately imperious manner. Whereupon he came out, shoved two bob in my hand and told me to piss off. When I angrily returned the money and told him that I wanted to buy the Jaguar, he said I'd need a bigger deposit than two bob and stalked back to his cubicle. I got the feeling that you needed to be wearing decorations, to have a letter from a vicar and a urine sample before you'd be considered.

Nonetheless, the Jag-wah (as owners call them) was a

great success and became the first of many. For after the sedan came the E-type, that most elegant fiacre. I felt little desire to drive it fast as, to me, it was a piece of sculpture. So much so that I regretted my inability to park it in the loungeroom. God, but I pampered that preposterous machine. That is, until a middle-aged lady on her way to a funeral (cross my heart) rammed it in her Hillman Minx. She emerged unscathed from the encounter and proceeded to chase the cortege while my E-type looked like a crushed cigarette pack.

But the high point in my absurd addiction, my shameless, irrational lust for cars, came with the purchase of a second-hand Maserati capable of 170 miles per hour. (I bought it from a racing driver who wanted something nippier.) Sad to say, on my first run in the country, something very funny happened to the engine. Not funny ha-ha so much as funny tragic. It had to be towed to the mechanic's where it remained for six long months while the Italians considered whether or not they'd send the spare parts. Finally, in outrage, I rang the Italian Embassy and actually bullied my way through to the Ambassador. What hope, I asked him, was there for Italian exports if people couldn't get their spare parts for their Maseratis? '*Signor,*' he said quietly, 'I drive a Fiat and I cannot get parts. So on my trips to Roma, I smuggle them back in my diplomatic bag.' What could I say? We sobbed quietly together for a while, murmured moist '*ciaos,*' and rang off.

When the wretched thing was finally fixed, I had to drive to David Williamson's for a script conference on *Don's Party,* only to discover that David lived among cultured hill-billies in a sort of Dogpatch outside Eltham, in a virtually unexplored region where Aborigines often speared the milkman. Worse still, the ruts in the roads were as deep as mineshafts and by the time I'd arrived at his eyrie, the Maserati's stainless steel entrails had been strewn for miles. It felt like a video replay of *The Cars that Ate Paris* with

41

hints from *Picnic at Hanging Rock* insofar as the ancient landscape devoured the out-of-time interloper.

A few follies later, I took delivery of a new sports sedan from Britain. Given the comments I'm about to make, I'll leave it unnamed for fear of legal action or of being roughed up by some wide boys from Soho. Suffice to say that my new car is the last of the dinosaurs, a fuel-guzzling fiasco that is already an anachronism, a sort of futuristic fossil. (As I pass service stations, grateful owners run out and cheer.) Well, it arrived by boat a few weeks back and seemed to have been used as a doss house by at least three stowaways. As well as the remains of meals and cigarette butts, the body was liberally measled with dents and paint chips. But after a few days in the paint shop, it emerged as comely as the photographs.

Although I soon discovered the following defects. The bonnet didn't close properly, nor did the boot. The passenger door could not be opened from the inside while the doors could not be locked for the lack of the appropriate key. The map lights and interior lights didn't work, while both the electric clock and the air-conditioner were kaput. But then, my new car was a folly and it's a point of honour for follies to be impractical. Pooh-poohing the shortcomings as mere bagatelles, I prepared to enjoy my first ride in what was, what is a car of remarkable grace, a model enthusiastically endorsed by *Road and Track, Car and Driver,* and the well-known mattress authority, Peter Wherrett.

Easing myself into the seat, I soon heard the exciting sound of 'vroom, vroom', issuing from both the engine and my mouth. With tremulous anticipation I eased out into the traffic and was soon burbling along in fine style. When, out of the blue, one of those cement trucks with a huge revolving thing on the back, decided to change lanes without signals or any apparent reason. Unless, perhaps, it was a vehement act of social criticism. Whereupon the front mudguard and the passenger door of my triumph of technology was cruelly crumpled. Oblivious of or indifferent to the incident the truck continued on its brutish way, its cement mixer twirling. This provoked me into a rage-filled chase worthy of Starsky and Hutch. Within moments I'd tooted and waved the behemoth to the kerb and had climbed out ready to slap the driver on the cheek with my chamois and to challenge him to an immediate duel with spanners.

But the bloke who slowly emerged from the cabin was no ordinary truck driver. He was as big and hairy as the gorilla that swings from the Empire State Building swatting at tiger moths. And if *he* was off-putting, you should have seen his big brother who climbed out of the other door.

Cringing and obsequious, I apologised for running my vulgar new car into the side of their sensible cement truck and offered to pay for any damages. If need be, I'd buy them a new truck. A new truck *each*. Walking backwards, I kicked another dent into my car just to demonstrate how lightly I'd taken the entire incident and told them to feel free to express themselves at any time. I also stressed that I voted Labor, supported republicanism and looked forward to the time when the guillotines were operating in Toorak. Then emitting a loud 'vroom, vroom', I was off up the road to safety. If only I hadn't forgotten the car.

In Greek, Phillip means lover of horses. But I don't even *like* horses. Great smelly things that tread on you. On the other hand, I'd been gripped by this insatiable passion for horse-power, for the infernal combustion engine. But this week's experience has finally convinced me that I must leave cars alone, just as the alcoholic must shun the bottle. Which is why I came to my agreement with the truckies. They now deliver their concrete in my sports sedan while I feel unassailable in their truck. On the one hand its hard to park, but that big, revolving boot is great for the shopping.

Superfluous
Superman

Fame is as ephemeral as fairy floss. Like spun sugar melting in the mouth, it melts in the mind. The moving finger of a Johnny Ray or Victor Mature writes autographs, and having writ moves on. To flog real estate in Florida or insurance in New York.

What happened to . . . ? There are so many Missing Persons in the overcrowded files of memory. The fallen stars, the failed politicians, the forgotten writers. Even the most soaring of celebrities – I refer of course to Superman – has gone with the wind. This is a most serious matter. Are we so ungrateful for his efforts against evil, for his titanic battles on behalf of the American Way? Consider for a moment the inspirational role he played for my generation.

Which gives me a long-awaited opportunity to mention *Adams with Added Enzymes* the only book to be remaindered before the ink was dry. Having sunk immediately on launching, it was ignored by literary editors, by the book trade and by their customers. (As a result it's now as rare as the folio Shakespeare or the Gutenberg Bible.) This is unfortunate, as the foreword, among other things, restated my theory about the theological significance of Superman.

Though despised for their trashiness and worthlessness, I defend comics as the fairy stories, the parables of the industrial age. Consider the way unfamiliar myths are restated, the ugly duckling living on in the puny schoolboys who became bullet-proof giants. My memory is defective on the details, but I seem to remember the crippled new boy Billy Batson conjuring Captain Marvel with the cry SHAZAM, a mystic acronym for Solomon, Hercules, Atlas, Zeus, Archimedes and Mercury. Then there were the interesting parallels between the stories of Christ and of Superman. Just as Three Wise Men found their way to the stable, Mr and Mrs Kent followed a falling star that led them to a rocket-powered crib. As with the crib in Bethlehem this contained a gift from the heavens – an extraordinary child who grew up to be something of a saviour.

Just as the Son of God took the improbable form of a humble carpenter, Superman was hidden in the identity of Clark Kent, mild-mannered journalist. Neither character showed much interest in the opposite sex (look at the way Clark fobbed off Lois Lane) and both had a way of coming down on sinners like a ton of bricks. While Christ was single-handedly clearing crooked financiers from the temple, Superman was vaulting tall buildings in a single leap to apprehend bank robbers. And here's another significant point: Superman's Mum was called Mary. 'Now listen to me Clark,' she'd say, 'this strength of yours, you've got to hide it from people. And when the proper time comes, you must use it to assist humanity'.

45

So much for theology. In a sociological sense, Superman stood for Imperial America, for the US of Lindberg, MacArthur, Dulles and Johnson. As much as the statue on Ellis Island, as the mighty portraits of Mt Rushmore and as your average John Wayne movie, Superman was the embodiment of the USA's grandiose self image. That is, until the patriotic puffery that sustained the super power gave way to despair and America began to pucker like a leaking zeppelin.

This, of course, occurred when the USA refused to learn the lessons of the mighty dinosaur which sank so stupidly into primeval swamps. For America proceeded to get itself bogged to the axles in Asia's rice paddies. Just one more case of too much brawn, too little brain. Where did the humiliations of Vietnam leave the old-style heroes? Up the well-known creek without a paddle, that's where. While the Pentagon put its wild Westmorelands out to pasture, Hollywood forced John Wayne to parody his old heroics. Retrenched from biblical epics, Charlton Heston was forced to make a monkey of himself on the Planet of the Apes.

Meanwhile the full-throated bellowings of Frankie Laine and Tex Ritter gave way to the self-pitying whines of Woodstock. And then the comic strips, the might of the masked marvels yielded to the pathos of Peanuts and the cynicism of the Wizard of Id. But the most tragic volte-face was that of Superman. Following my recent visit to Metropolis and my investigations at the Daily Planet, I have to report that my childhood hero is now a tragic figure.

Right through the War and Cold War years, Superman and Clark Kent not only fought all forms of wickedness but set brats like myself a splendid example. But in a world of pappous protest, their method of upholding law and order began to look absurdly short-back-and-sides. Superman was eclipsed by Abbie Hoffman, Rap Brown and Peter Fonda. And Superman wasn't the only one to suffer. Captain Marvel was seriously injured in a collision with a cropduster over

Kansas while Batman was arrested for the seduction of a minor, a scandal that rocked conservative Gotham City.

. But the bigger they are, the harder they fall. Out of work for weeks on end, our hero scanned the employment columns for someone, anyone needing a man of his special powers.

Finally Superman was hired, on trial, by radio station WXCV in Los Angeles to give aerial road reports. 'And now it's up, up and away,' the DJ would say, 'to our flying fool and his freeway report! Come in, Super-baby.' Whereupon our intrepid birdman would warn of the bank-up on a free-way while suggesting alternatives for commuters. However, being called Super-baby and such-like by a 90-mile-an-hour mouth wreaked havoc with his sense of dignity. But some-how Superman stuck it out. What finally grounded our hero were scathing attacks from environmentalists who criticised him for causing damage when breaking the sound barrier. Furthermore they speculated that his tendency to leave vapour trails and dandruff in the stratosphere might damage the ozone layer and precipitate an Ice Age.

'I can jump 18-storey buildings in a single leap,' Super-man muttered morosely as he pushed his way through the dole's doleful line-up. 'That's great, Mac. But don't jump the queue,' came the sour rejoinder.

Then, for a while, things looked up. Superman was signed for Heinz Health Food ads. and had to do exercises on a day-time women's show. But he looked incongruous in the world of yoga and yoghurt and his contract wasn't renewed. 'Frankly,' said Central Casting, 'you're *passé.*'

Dragging himself from the office, Superman reconsidered his position. This was a time for drastic action. So drastic action is what he took. And when he represented himself at Central Casting a few weeks later he'd redecorated his chest with a new, psychedelic S. He'd had his cape drasti-cally restyled by Cardin. And he'd invested in a new, Sas-soon hairstyle. But even this failed to rekindle the public interest. So Superman found himself applying to Universal for work as a movie stuntman.

'Clearly,' said the studio, 'you haven't been to the movies lately. These days all the best heroes die in a hail of bullets. Everyone's cut down in their prime. Blood everywhere. So frankly, who needs a bullet-proof stuntman?'

Nor could Superman expect much help from his alter-ego at the Daily Planet. Because of the economic downturn in Metropolis, advertising revenue had been halved. So editor Perry White was given to drunken lunches at the Playboy Club. Meanwhile cub reporter Jimmy Olsen had become a junky and Lois Lane, having long evidenced a withering contempt for males in general and Clark Kent in particular, was working with Gloria Steinem on a women's lib magazine.

You didn't need x-ray eyes to see the writing on the wall. Clark Kent handed in his press card and joined the public relations firm where he lobbied the local legislature and wrote hand-outs for Bell Telephone. And every time he saw a photograph of a phone booth, grief would mist his glasses.

Now I come to the final pathetic page in the Superman story. Given such a hopeless and humiliating situation, it is surely permissible for a man to shake his fist at the heavens and say 'No!' It is surely permissible, even admirable, for such a man to renounce his own life.

Then spare a thought for Superman who, for weeks, has been trying unsuccessfully to do away with himself. Every bullet he shoots ricochets from his unpunctured person. And when he hurls himself from the tops of tall buildings, he just floats.

Is it a bird? Is it a plane? No, it's Superman. Superseded, superannuated, superfluous.

A schoolboy's language

Forget the CIA, the television set is the main tool of American imperialism and subversion. Take the way American colloquialisms continue to make inroads into our ocker vocab. So today I'm recording some of the indigenous slang employed at my state school lest it be lost forever. Parents sharing my concern should remove this article and have their children memorise its contents, along with the catechism and Lord's Prayer.

Nicky woop: To go away hurriedly.

Catholic dogs sitting on logs: A chant sung on the school bus to kids in navy blue jumpers.

State, state, fulla hate: A chant sung by kids with navy blue jumpers to kids wearing grey jumpers.

POQ: See nicky woop.

Ooh Aah! You're going to get into it: You're about to incur the wrath of the administration.

Ooh Aah! I'm going to tell on you: I will inform the authorities.

You fat pimp!: The standard response to 'I'm going to tell on you.'

Copy cat: An unoriginal person or someone who cribs during exams, thus necessitating covering one's work with a cupped hand.

'Miss Beckett, Robert Milburn poked his tongue out at you': A typical statement from someone who wants to suck up to the teacher.

49

Suck up: To crawl.

You're gonna get the cuts from Mr Dunstan: You'll be given corporal punishment by the headmaster.

Who wacked off with my alley-bag?: Who stole my marble holder?

Tombowlers, blood reels and cats eyes: Things kept in an alley bag.

A fnudger: A poor stylist at alleys.

Fannany-wacking: Cribbing at alleys.

Got you a bewdy: To succeed in one-up-kid-ship, as in the following exchange. 'Do you know what?' 'What?' 'You're mad and I'm not! Ha ha ha!'

Doing lines: Being kept in to write out good resolutions, such as 'I must not put squashed frogs in girls' sandwiches'. The more skilful kid was able to expedite matters by writing with three pens at once.

Roger Fraser, Graham Stobey, Peter Radcliffe, Judy Stubbs and Colin O'Rourke: Some of my friends in third grade.

I'll get Rourky to bash you up: I'll ask Colin O'Rourke to hit you in return for dosh.

Dosh: Money.

Choo-Choo bars: A hard licorice confection that cost real dosh. That is, threepence.

Yonnie: A stone.

Brinnie: A stone a bit smaller than a yonnie, as used in brinnie fights.

A ging: A shanghai used to propel brinnies or yonnies.

Packawackers: A group of school fellows showing evidence of intellectual impairment.

'Give us a look at yours and I'll give you a look at mine.': Let's have a reciprocal genital inspection.

Rourky got his temper up - ha ha ha!: Colin O'Rourke is showing signs of vexation.

Orright - who wacked off with me collars?: Who stole my Derwent coloured pencils?

Swappies: Playing cards depicting kittens, ballet dancers and such like.

Jacks: A game played with meat-knuckle bones.

Knuckles: A more violent game with one's own knuckle bones.

Hoppo-Bumpo: A game played by hopping around on one leg, using folded arms as bumper bars.

Oompah, oompah stick it up your joompah: A contemptuous retort.

Bum: The rudest word in the primary school vocabulary.

Putting up your hand: A gesture to signify that you know the answer to teacher's question or, more likely, that you have an urgent desire to visit the dunny.

Triangle: A musical instrument used by the bubs.

Brandy: A ball game involving being 'branded' with viciously tossed tennis balls.

Bend-your-bum Curve-your-arse: The nick-name given to Mr Benjamin Nankervis, one of my favourite teachers.

Sissy: An effeminate person.

Ink monitors, prefects and house captains: See crawler or suck-up.

Dinkys: Small, highly desirable model cars.

Dinks: Uncomfortable rides on the seat or cross-bar of a Malvern Star or Healing.

Getting picked: Awaiting selection by the captain of any team game, an interminable and humiliating experience.

Getting picked on: Being bullied or victimised.

Spit balls: A projectile made by chewing blotter and then dipping it in ink. It could then be flicked considerable distances with one's ruler.

Ruler: A wooden device for filling grooves in your desk or for flicking spitballs.

Compass: A device for picking warts, having first medicated them with ink.

Cut lunch: Stale sandwiches made for you by a loving mother which you did your best to either lose or swap.

Bought lunch: Fresh sandwiches made at the lolly shop; considered vastly superior.

Oslo lunch: An unhappy compromise between the cut lunch

and the bought lunch available from the school tuck shop.

Sherbet suckers: Paper bags full of an effervescent chemical inhaled through a licorice straw.

Clinkers: Torpedo-shaped chocolate-covered confections.

Water bombs: A practical application of origami.

Waggin' it: Being absent without leave.

Having a note: A document, frequently forged, providing an alibi for when you'd wagged it.

Break-up day: The end of term when you handed in your locker key and sang the following ditty: 'no more spelling, no more books, no more teachers with dirty looks'.

Getting the needles: Being inoculated against TB, polio or other social diseases.

Camphor bags: Mystic talismans worn around the neck during the polio scare.

Emperor gum moth caterpillar: A much sought after technicolour grub found on pepper-corn trees.

School bags: Receptable for rotten bananas, old lunches, Superman comics and pencil cases. When swung by the straps, a highly effective weapon.

Yabbies: Fresh water crustaceans lured from muddy dams with lumps of rancid meat tethered to pieces of string. A delicacy second only to the Choo-Choo Bar.

Bikes: The standard means of transport.

Semi-racer: The most desirable form of bike, fitted with a dynamo, pack-rack and Sturmey-Archer gears.

Education day: An opportunity for parents to feign interest in your progress.

Inner tubes: Indispensable for making gings and lacker guns. Also useful when swimming in the dam.

Assembly: A crypto-fascist ritual wherein one swore allegiance to God, King, country and other manifestations of the Establishment.

Itchy powder: A material obtained from the seed-pods of a tree commonly planted by municipal councils.

Play lunch: Emergency rations for morning recess, usually being a piece of fruit, cake or some chocolate crackles.

Chocolate crackles: Home-made confection of rice bubbles and copha.

Opportunity grade: The ironic title given by the Education Department to a hopeless class full of backward children.

Bubs: Kids under five.

Big kids: Kids over ten.

Wanna get bashed up?: A threat of imminent violence.

You and who's army?: A show of unconcern.

Religious instruction: Bedlam.

Out of bounds: Almost everywhere.

Chewie: The universal adhesive found under desks and shoes.

Koala and Elephant stamps: Rewards for high academic achievement.

Smartie: See skite.

Skite: See show-off.

Show off: An arrogant, extroverted person.

PT: Physical torture.

Stacking the lockers: Piling up books in such a way as to cause an avalanche when an unsuspecting classmate opens the door.

Bags: Not to be confused with school bag; a method of staking a claim as in 'I bags that'.

You're he: The special status given to someone who's been tigged or who's turn it is to count up to fifty in hidee.

Coming ready or not: The cry of whoever's he, usually emitted when they've counted to about thirty.

Smokey Dawson: A childhood hero on the radio and Kellogg's packets.

Houses: The school's regiments, named after obscure figures in parochial history.

Lollie money: Dosh kept in the corner of a hankie.

I know your girl-friend: A derisive chant.

Tossel: The male member.

Whissy-dicks: The female pudenda.

Sent out of the room: Being banished for misconduct, such as painting your tossel in art class.

Sent to the head: The result of even worse misconduct.

Getting the strap: A stinging blow to the upturned palm as a result of being sent to the head.

Who fluffed?: An enquiry regarding flatulence.

The day
of the dragon
in a child's world

When I was a child, and thought as a child, I gazed up at grown-ups with a mixture of exasperation and determination. I was exasperated by their ineptitude with children, with their impatience at our problems and their inability to comprehend a three-foot-six-inch point of view. So I was determined to remember exactly what it felt like to be a kid, so that I might, one day, be a more successful parent.

Unhappily I did not keep that resolution. As the tempo of adult life caught me up, I'd less and less time for their questions, games and fantasies. Like my parents, I became authoritarian, too often rapping out commands like some self-important sergeant-major. I became what most parents become; a benevolent bully.

The net result is that children can seem as mysterious and inscrutable as Tibetans or Martians. Which is why they make such convincing monsters in upper-class horror films like *Children of the Damned*. If they're honest, most adults are thoroughly discomforted by kids because they don't know what they're thinking, what judgments are being made behind those bright, bland eyes.

More than once, during America's endless campaign for racial equality, a white journalist had disguised himself as a black and written an account of his experiences in the Deep South. Of the humiliation of being ordered out of restaurants, of being forced to sit in the back of a bus, of being called 'boy' and denied employment. Similarly it might be

55

an object lesson for adults to walk around on their knees for a week or so, not in some painful penitence but so as to be reminded of a child's Lilliputian perspective.

Of late I've found another way of remembering. It involves reading the writings of the very young. If nothing else it brushes away the crowded sentiments that fog an adult's vision, revealing children for what they are: captivating primitives.

Take the following essays, by a group of migrant kids. They were asked to describe their reaction to a dragon masticating one or more of their family. Most of the children advocated immediate capital punishment. Take Terry's vivid scenario.

One day are dragon came to my house and to eat my sester and I thout the dragon wheel eat my famyl and the dragon was gon rrrr and a chop in his tall and he was keld.

Echoing this idea is Mick who put it this way.

One day a dragon ate me sister. I will chop his tail off. He will not have a taill.

As for Vicki, she put it more simply.

I wood get a sord and after I will kily him at the stumik.

However, one child staged a battle worthy of St. George. Presumably his penchant for violence developed as a result of prolonged exposure to television.

I jump on him and I puchet in and he puchet me on the back and he eats my brother and I will pray kung fu and he punchet me tand I got anger and I punchet and I got the nife and kill him.

Just as vindictive was Mahmut who said:

If a dragon came and ate me brother I will kill he at nite when he is a slept. I will kill he with the nife and bruck his bons.

Not all the kids were simply out for vengeance. Some wished to save their loved ones and advocated more sophisticated surgery.

In one gulp he swallow my brother. Then I ran to the draw and got my fifteen inches knife. If tried to spitt its tumy open and I did. Out jumped my baby brother he ran to me and said qa fa ta (which mean thank you) we took the dragon to the museuem and I kept it tail and it teeth. Then I broke it bones.

Another little boy was just as sure of grateful thanks.

If a dragon comes in my house, I will kill him whith a knife and My Mum will love me.

But it isn't all sweetness and light, with one child positively inviting disaster. While his tenses are uncertain his sentiments are unequivocal.

A dragon liv acros the road. I wish he ate up my little sister and I woulden care a bit. I would ask him for a ride on his back and he gives me a ride it was smooth and I like going fast.

One child in the group considered the possibility of turning the tables and eating the dragon.

When I went to bed a dragon came into my house and I shoped is head of and I had his head for my tea.

Then there was a kid who approached the whole thing more matter-of-factly. As his experience of life told him that the meek did *not* inherit the earth, he wrote:

One there was a dragon he lived in a cave. And kill my sister and brother, mother and father and the dragon lived happily every after.

However, my favourite essay says it all in a single sentence. Instead of attacking stumiks or taills, this child got straight to the point.

If the dragons ate my futtr I will chop his dick off with a nife . . .

'If these were the best years of our lives, why did we feel so caged?'

SPOONER.

Childhood was a totalitarian régime from which I was very glad to escape. Still, we sentimentalise that time, remembering it as so many sandcastles and party balloons. Too often we remember ourselves running through long grass in slow motion, with a dog at our side, like in those lyrical television commercials for cornflakes. Yet childhood was a time of indignities and injustice. A few days ago I saw a typical scene. A mother was dragging a tired child through a big store and he was lagging, dragging. Whereupon she suddenly flared and belted him repeatedly on the backside, causing his weariness to become tears and cries of outrage. Needless to say this embarrassed the mother all the more, so she hit him harder.

That was one of the worst aspects of childhood, the fact that a kid was property. Indeed, the dominant memory of childhood was being ordered about by parents, teachers, prefects, bullies. What were school assemblies but miniature Nuremberg rallies where pompous, petty officials could indulge their egos? I well remember the way the more paranoid teachers lorded it over their diminutive, powerless populations dressed in their compulsory uniforms.

But it was just as bad at home. One was ordered to wash one's hands, clean one's teeth or to kiss some overscented friend of mummy's whose gush of affection was manifestly insincere. Then there was the way you were sent to bed just when things were getting interesting or were forced to endure the ignominy of short pants. Don't ask silly questions. Just do what you're told. Don't answer back. How dare you talk to your mother like that? If children were to be seen and not heard, adults were to be obeyed and not questioned.

You were subject to various forms of martial law, including the curfew, and had no right of appeal. There were no political parties to represent you, no trade union to protect you. You had to eat your spinach, your pumpkin and your words. Again and again grown-ups would tell us how lucky we were to be young, urging us to enjoy our childhood while we could. And most of the time this sounded to be the ravings of lunatics, given our desperation to shake off the yoke of youth. Most of us would have gladly chucked our childhood away, which is why we were so anxious to get into long pants and out of school. To us the fence around the playground was like the Berlin Wall, with teachers substituting for the provosts with their machine guns.

Then there was the ugly side to our personalities. I well remember the poor mongoloid child who lived in a flat above the local bank. On the way home from school we'd find him on the swings in the park or hanging from the rusty chains of the iron maypole. We'd begin by just talking to him, laughing at him, forcing him to answer stupid questions like a trained cockatoo. But then our goading would become cruel and we'd start to hit him. Yet he was too amiable to run away. After all these years I can still see the hurt and confusion in his eyes. And at the time I felt a vague unease and guilt about it, but it didn't stop me from doing it again.

Another dimension of our cruelty was the way we'd pick on those post-war unfortunates, the migrant kids. The term 'New Australian' had to be forced into our vocabulary and remains as ludicrous as the euphemism 'national serviceman' for conscript. Yet it was certainly better than the epithet of reffo or DP. 'Go back to your own country,' we'd chant at some bewildered victim.

Of course the pecking order in a schoolyard is as vicious as that of a fowlyard. The bullying is stratified in exactly the same way with some poor little bastard being the ultimate victim. He might be weak or weak-minded or particularly shabbily dressed. If he was especially vulnerable, he'd be the target. Years later I read *Lord of the Flies,* and when the kids killed poor Piggy it had the unmistakable ring of truth.

As well as being racist and religious bigots, kids are also

snobs. I well remember times in class when we'd turn our attention to the poorest, most neglected child present; to someone who came to school in hand-me-downs, looking just a little dirtier than the rest of us. One such child, a girl called Val, was nicknamed Stinky by us all and her life must have been a crucifixion. For my own part, I suffered the nickname of Boofhead, and, although my cranium was only slightly larger than the normal, I felt as though it were a dirigible.

While I remember some of my teachers with affection and gratitude, I remember others with detestation. It's amazing the number of classroom sadists I encountered, worse bullies than any you'd find in the playground.

And I also remember the agonisingly slow progress of the classroom clock. Nowadays an hour seems a minute, a week lasts a day. But then time was interminable. Every class seemed a life sentence. I also remember the turgid rhetoric of Anzac Day speeches and the pompous lyrics of school songs. (Fancy being forced to sing stupid verses about one's undying debt to a group of prefab classrooms and a patch of broken asphalt.) Then there was the hollow mockery of the flag ceremony: 'I love God, I love God and my country, I will honour the flag, I will serve my King and cheerfully obey my parents, teachers and the laws.' And they talk of indoctrination on mainland China and tut-tut about Chairman Mao's *Little Red Book*.

Then there was the tyranny of sport, of the compulsory worship of football. And because I was no good at it, I was one of the poor devils that waited and waited to be picked for sides. Two of those odious school heroes (most of them finished up on points duty or as unsuccessful commercial travellers – there's a certain vindictive pleasure in that), would stand out in front and choose the kids they wanted, like Southern gentlemen at a slave auction. A barbarous system, because someone had to be last.

Then there was the tyranny of ignorance, not knowing

61

about things. Of being curious about sex and not being told. I can remember one day hearing a boy I rather admired – I think his name was Lindsay Shields – saying a funny word in the school ground. For some reason it struck me as an amusing group of letters. After all, duck was funny and so this word was funnier still. While I had no idea as to its meaning, it stuck in my mind and, that night, when cleaning my shoes, I was chanting it to myself. Whereupon my grandmother came charging through the door like a Valkyrie and boxed my ears, thus branding the word for ever in my vocabulary.

Of course, there were good things like Crosbie Morrison's nature broadcasts and hearing Grandpa and his mates sing their favourite songs like *The Rugged Cross* and *The Galloping Major.* And being given a few legs to crack from the crayfish which in those days was working man's food.

But for the most part childhood was crushing boredom. It was sitting on a kerb writing down the numbers of trams or the number-plates of cars as they came and went. It was swapping comics that you'd read twice already. It was being so limited in finance and freedom that one's options were pitifully narrow. It was being told to put on a jumper, to stay in the backyard, to do one's homework. It was being required to mow the lawn weekend after weekend, a task that seemed absurdly repetitive and ultimately meaningless.

And, increasingly, it was coping with the sufferings of puberty. Most of the time when I was a kid I felt myself on the receiving end of adult indifference or incompetence. And I remember pledging that I would be different when I grew up, that I would remember what it meant to be a kid. Yet when I think of my own impatience with my children, I know that I've forgotten.

Into another dimension

Some clues to the truth behind *Picnic at Hanging Rock*

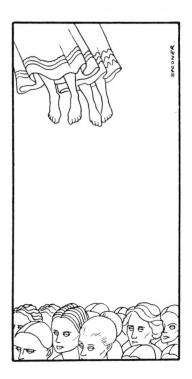

Picnic at Hanging Rock tells the story of a group of school-girls who, for once, manage to escape strict supervision and climb the paths that wind among the looming tors of an extinct volcano. Three of them disappear, as does their somewhat eccentric maths teacher. And the repercussions of this inexplicable event are a succession of tragedies. Few people reading Joan Lindsay's novel have solved its mystery, although all the clues are there. The trouble is that no Hercule Poirot spends the last chapter standing in a drawing room or railway carriage plaiting the loose ends into a noose for the butler. Or whoever. Joan preferred to leave her narrative enigmatic, tantalising.

I'm told there's a secret chapter, one that explains all. But Joan withdrew it from the manuscript and has, ever since, refused to release it. Instead she adds to the mystery, and amuses herself by giving pestiferous interviewers and theses writers generous servings of red herring.

For example, Joan hints that the incident might be based on fact, thus sending them off on fruitless searches through newspaper files. Yet they can't say they weren't warned, as the frontispiece carries this note:

> Whether the story is fact or fiction my readers must decide for themselves. As the fateful picnic took place in the year 1900, and all the characters who appear in this book are long since dead, it hardly seems important.

When pressured about it, she'll seem genuinely uncertain, blaming a failing memory. Or she'll change tracks, shrugging her shoulders as she wonders whether something imagined isn't as real as what the unimaginative call reality.

As well as eliminating some of the book's deaths and disasters, the film removes a number of Joan's specific clues. However, it replaces them with hints of its own. Where the book is written in a low key and somewhat ironic style, a style that distances the reader from the mounting toll, the film (and it's a *marvellous* film) is almost a ballet in which doomed, romantic people move as in a dream, where Hanging Rock rises in the landscape to ominous organ music, like a satanic Wurlitzer.

But while the film continually hints at the mystical, audiences persist in looking for Hector Crawford solutions, for rational explanations. 'That boy from England,' you hear people saying after a screening, 'he killed them.' Well, he didn't. Nobody killed them. I'm certain I know what happened and will, in due course, reveal it. But first it's necessary to talk about Joan Lindsay and her attitude to life and time – for it was through knowing Joan that I found the clues leaping from the page.

No, I haven't been privy to any confidences on the matter. But I believe that the book springs as much from Joan's philosophies as it does from her experiences around the turn

64

of the century at her girls' school at Mt Macedon. It's also necessary to talk about Hanging Rock itself, for I regard it as the most important character in the mystery.

Like Joan, I've long been drawn to Hanging Rock. Many years before I'd read the book, I'd made two films there myself, one about a doomed love affair, the other about death. I know of no more evocative setting. Even before that, as a child, I explored Hanging Rock on many occasions, looking for the bush-rangers' gold (taken from coaches en route to Melbourne from the goldfields, as they travelled through the nearby Black Forest) which legend has hidden deep in the labyrinth. For me the volcanic ruin of Hanging Rock really was the Rock of Ages, the most ancient and profound of places.

As a child I was also drawn to a picture of the edifice in the National Gallery. Called 'Picnic Day at Hanging Rock', it was painted by one William Ford in 1875. (And remember that Joan's husband, Sir Daryl Lindsay, was the Director of that gallery for many years.) It hangs among a number of pre-Heidelberg paintings, all of which show the unease that 19th century artists, and their fellow citizens, felt about the antipodean landscape. Because it was so different from the domesticated, hospitable vistas of England, they painted our skies as if they were English skies. And as well as softening the light, they'd turn gum trees into oak trees so they'd feel less estranged and threatened.

Ford's painting shows these traits. At the same time, it depicts the same paradox that the film emphasises – the extraordinary sight of elegant, crinolined figures against such an ominous and alien backdrop. Not even the Great Pyramid, which rises from the desert as abruptly as Hanging Rock does from the surrounding plains, is more charged with significance. These are the bones of pre-history breaking through the thin soil. These are Aboriginal rocks, dreamtime rocks. Bunyip lairs.

In a way the people in the painting and the characters

both in the novel and in the film, seem out of place and out of time. Revisiting the painting this morning, I was reminded of the short stories of E M Forster, where the odd English tourist (more sensitive than his fellow travellers) falls under the ancient spell of the Greek landscape and finds himself in the thrall of Pan or Bacchus. And this paradox, this culture shock, is the first clue to Joan's mystery.

The second clue is the day of the picnic, St Valentine's Day. Quite by coincidence we had the Lindsays for dinner last Valentine's Day and discovered it was their umpteenth anniversary. As well, Joan treasures a collection of St Valentine's cards dating back to childhood – and a collection of memories to go with them. St Valentine's Day is her magic day, when the commonplace is overwhelmed by the extraordinary.

The third clue concerns the references to the hours and years that crowd the text. As well as awed talk of the rock's million years, we hear Miranda's (Joan's?) philosophy about time: 'Miranda used to say,' says Irma, the missing girl who reappears just as mysteriously as she disappeared, 'that everything begins and ends at exactly the right time and place . . .'

Moreover there's the odd way that everyone's watch stops at noon, just as they arrive at the rock's vicinity. Consider the fact that Joan's autobiography was called *Time Without Clocks,* and that there are no clocks at Mulberry Hill, the Lindsays' home. Joan says she cannot wear a watch, that they simply stop on her wrist, that she has the same odd effect on the watches of her friends. More importantly, like J B Priestley, Joan believes that times present, times past and times future co-exist, that time isn't the simplistic continuum that most of us believe. Long before Einstein revealed his relativity theory, in which time ceases to be something solid and dependable and becomes elastic, Joan believed that it was somehow dreamlike, that yesterday is still with us while tomorrow is already here.

66

Let's summarise the clues to this point. The picnic occurs on a day of mysticism and myth, at a place where the characters are at odds with the landscape, on a day when watches stop, when even the coach-driver is uncertain as to the hour. When a girl who talks of time in a curious, ambivalent way leads her friends up a winding path into the future.

I believe that the mystery is revealed, becomes self-evident at this point. The girls climb higher and higher up the rock. They shed their shoes and stockings, just as their maths teacher (who disappears quite separately) is seen to remove her skirt. Just as the surviving girl is found without her corset. Needless to say the police give such disrobing a sinister, sexual connotation. But for me it symbolises the removal of constraint, the shedding of unimaginative disciplines.

As the girls move towards the peak, Joan has them look down at the picnickers 'through a drift of rosy smoke, or mist'. This 'pink cloud' is described again, by the fat girl who flees her entranced friends, preferring the safety of numbers. However, it is dismissed by the investigators as being too fanciful and absurd.

'Whatever can those people be doing down there, like a lot of ants?' says Marion. 'A surprising number of human beings are without purpose.' And just as those lines are sinking into the reader's mind, lines that suggest the girls may be making some sort of choice between meaningless reality and a fascinating dream, the key words – and the book's most important clue – occur.

> Irma was aware, for a little time, of a rather curious sound coming up from the plain. Like the beating of far-off drums.

Hours later, in *real time,* the searchers will be beating sticks on sheets of tin. Yet the girls hear those sounds already while, below them, the picnic continues undisturbed. It's as simple as that, and as complex. No wonder the bloodhounds lose the trail. For the girls aren't lost on the rock. Like Alices stepping through the looking glass, they're moving into another dimension.

A week later, after the most elaborate search, one of the girls is found sleeping near the peak quite unharmed except for a few scratches on her face and hands. At the time the police are puzzled by the absence of scratches on her bare feet. They cannot know that she's been walking in time, not on the rock. And for some reason that neither she nor us can know, she's returned.

Consider Joan's (Miranda's?) philosophy. Everything begins and ends at the right time and place, yet all time co-exists. Thus the girls choose to leave shoes and stockings, a life 'purpose' and St Valentine's Day 1900 behind them. And if Joan is right about time, they may still be on Hanging Rock. They could come walking down the path tomorrow.

I haven't discussed it with Joan, but I'm sure that this is the answer to the mystery that's puzzled readers since 1968 and will puzzle the thousands who have the good fortune to see Peter Weir's film. Mind you, there are other little mysteries. Why do the lost girls' names all begin with anagrams of the same four letters? Miranda, Irma, Marion. Is there some significance in the French mistress's sudden realisation that Miranda's face is identical to one in a Botticelli painting?

Just as mystics and eccentric mathematicians continue to find significances in the geometry or measurements of the Great Pyramid, others will find new puzzles at Joan Lindsay's Hanging Rock.

The film to beat them all

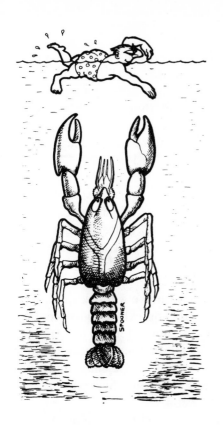

A few months ago, twenty miles off the coast of Port Lincoln in South Australia, an American midget called Carl Rizzo was lowered into the depths in a wire cage. His role? To be bait for a shark attack to be filmed by our very own Ron and Valerie Taylor. Mr Rizzo's diminutive size was not a consequence of cost-cutting as the film had an $8 million budget. Rather, he was to make any unfriendly piece of flake look larger and fiercer by comparison. And his ordeal was to be intercut with dramatic footage shot near Chappaquiddick, Teddy Kennedy's favourite watering place.

Within seconds the shark appeared. First it tore a chunk out of the Taylors' boat. Then it mauled the cable supporting Rizzo and sent his cage plummeting to the bottom. It is this

69

scene, among others, that has made *Jaws* the most amazing financial success in the greedy history of Hollywood.

And having seen the film, vengeful Americans are rushing to hire boats so that they can kill sharks. Such is the irrational hatred engendered by the movie that an ancient species may be eliminated, just as the fly disappeared from China after the orgy of swatting ordered by Chairman Mao.

Yet our detestation of the *Carcharas vulgaris* isn't very fair. In recorded history only a handful of people have been eaten by sharks, although a larger number have lost weight as the result of an encounter. The way I look at it is this: given mankind's vast appetite for seafood, it's only the odd serve of fish and chips getting its own back.

Ever alert for an opportunity to make a quick quid, I resolved to produce a similar film as quickly as possible. (We in the Australian film industry are not notorious for our originality.) To that end I had to find another creature capable of haunting the subconscious minds of the mass audience, another lurking Nemesis. So I began checking out the menagerie from Aardvark to Zebu.

Imagine my despair when I discovered that almost every form of flora and fauna, irrespective of its size or origin, has already been exploited. Elizabeth Taylor survived a stampede of pachyderms in *Elephant Walk* just as Richard Burton was to dodge pink ones throughout their marriage. Then there was Eleanor Parker and Charlton Heston down to their last can of Mortein as legions of ants marched towards them through *The Naked Jungle*. In *Willard,* the threat came from regiments of rats, while in Hitchcock's *The Birds,* Rod Taylor and Tippi Hedren all but drowned in the droppings of savage seagulls while dodging the talons of bible-black crows. On a larger scale we had *The Giant Claw,* featuring a sort of pterodactyl that went around ingesting aircraft. (Instead of birds being drawn into jet engines, we saw airliners sucked into its nostrils.)

Meanwhile, at the microscopic end of the scale, we've had *The Andromeda Strain,* a sort of measle from out of space that turned one's blood into a white flaky material reminiscent of dandruff or desiccated coconut.

And in films like *The Thing* and *Day of the Chrysalids* even the fruit shop turned against us, with savage cabbages and carnivorous sticks of celery paying mankind back for the millions of their ilk massacred for salads. Further researches show that dinosaurs have been done to death in any number of Japanese horror films or in adaptations of Jules Verne – just as the belfries of Beverly Hills are crowded with Transylvanian bats.

In any case, as a patriotic Australian film maker, I wanted to use a local species. But it seemed a bit hard to strike terror in an audience with the close-up of the amiable features of a wombat. Then someone played me a popular recording by some rural troubadour concerning a redback on a toilet seat. And it certainly conjured up a whole succession of cinematic possibilities – a series of close-ups of people caught with their pants down, lowering their pale, vulnerable buttocks towards the seat, quite unaware of the agonising fate that awaited them. Like the shark, there was something about the redback spider that gnawed at the subconscious, and there'd be no trouble weaving toilet seats into a plot, particularly with the gastro going around.

But then it hit me: the one Australian creature that could terrify the mass audience and electrify the box office. So I went into production with my answer to *Jaws.* Made with the $750 grant from the Experimental Film Fund, my epic is called *Claws* and it stars that most awesome of Antipodean creatures, the *Cherax,* otherwise known as the yabbie.

First of all, I went out and caught one of these fearsome creatures with my bare hands. Well, actually I caught it with a piece of meat tied to six feet of string in the dam at the back of my aunty's poultry farm. However, anyone who witnessed the struggle to get it ashore would have immediately recalled those epic scences in *The Old Man and the Sea.* Sweat poured from my brow and the string cut into the palms of my hands as I battled the might and tenacity of the yabbie. But finally I dragged it ashore and it lay there panting and heaving beneath its massive carapace. Four and a half inches of brute force.

Much of *Jaws* was filmed with a mechanical shark. None of that trickery for me. Almost all of *Claws* was filmed with real, live yabbies, with the yielding flesh of our actors exposed to the cruel talons of that prehistoric crustacean. And to add to our difficulties, because of their extremely low IQ yabbies proved impossible to train. Just as the dinosaur's brain was the size of a pigeon's egg, your average yabbie has no more intelligence than a typical Young Liberal.

I must admit that the underwater sequences in *Claws* aren't as good as those in *Jaws,* owing to the murky waters of aunty's dam. But I feel that this adds to the sense of threat and insecurity in the audience. For just as Nessy could lurch from the Loch at any moment, a great nipper could lunge out of the mustard-coloured depths and seize an unsuspecting appendage. And make no mistake. Once you've been seized by a yabbie it's not a pretty sight. They can pick a toe clean within weeks.

In the long annals of cinema I doubt whether there's been a more terrifying image than that of the attacking yabbie with its beady, black eyes. The claws wave around like pairs of pliers while the feelers lash the air like whips. The only trouble is that, even using midget actors, yabbies don't look very large. So towards the end I decided to rewrite the script so that my yabbies could be affected by nuclear fallout from the French tests.

Thus we finished up with a yabbie thirty feet tall, capable of climbing up on the Sydney Harbour Bridge and grabbing at passing Cessnas and chomping ferries. Now the film became really horrifying as people were plucked from li-los in their backyard pools. Or they'd romp into the Yarra for a swim only to be sliced in two by a monstrous claw. (In one of our best moments you see a torso thrashing around in the water while a pair of legs runs for help.)

What's more, I've thought of a terrific follow-up. A film about a giant boxing kangaroo that devastates the country. To save a lot of money on sets, we'll superimpose shots of him over the newsreel footage of Darwin. We go into production as soon as Jack Rennie has finished retraining Skippy.

Disastrous début

Recently the *Age* carried a photograph of your columnist, in frock coat and pince-nez, rehearsing with Sheila Helpmann for a scene in *The Getting of Wisdom*. As the accompanying report stated, Sheila was playing the major role of Mrs Gurley, the formidable headmistress of a prim and proper 19th century girls' school, while I was to be Dr Pughson, her master of mathematics. But it erred when it said this was my début as a thespian. I am no stranger to the stage. Indeed, the world of wings, scrim and flies, of *mise-en-scène* and *ingenue* are my second home. I've every reason to believe that only a quirk of fate has kept me from my rightful place in the pantheon of the profession, along with Abigail and Delvene Delaney.

It's just that a few small things went wrong along the way. A few little accidents on stage. An occasional fluffed line or missed cue. Take my debut at the age of five. It was in a concert featuring the children of the East Kew State School and took place on the stage of the Kew Town Hall in 1944.

I distinctly remember climbing on board the No. 48 tram in the company of my mother. I was dressed for bed and clutching my teddy. I'd never been on a tram in the dark before, let alone in my 'jamas, and I was conscious of everybody *looking*. But on getting off at the Kew Post Office beside the doric war memorial, I discovered that all the other kids from the bubs' grade were similarly attired. We were all very interested in each others' 'jamas and nighties.

I then have a vivid memory of being lined up in the wings and told to lead my classmates on to the stage, whereupon the kids from all the other classes would follow us. And once our serried ranks were formed we'd all sing *Jesus Wants Me For a Sunbeam* or *Jingle Bells* or something. But as soon as I led my little troup into the spotlight, to the thunderous applause of our respective parents, I was so overcome that I burst into song. As did my retinue.

As I understand it, the evening never fully recovered from this premature ejaculation and made me *persona non grata* with the headmistress, Miss Coultis, who spent the next three years impounding my Dinky toys in revenge.

I got very, very few bookings in the subsequent years. It's true that I played William Tell in an improvised playlet in 2B and was one of the Argonauts in 3B when Lindsay Shields got the plum part of Jason and was tied to an imaginary pole while all the girls made seductive siren-type noises. Unfortunately, they confused Homer's sirens with police sirens, so the noise was deafening. However, Lindsay thrashed around and moaned quite commendably until we extras rowed him out of earshot. But this sexist drama, like the William Tell production, would have to be regarded as off-off-Broadway and I remained shunned whenever it came to casting a school concert. This is why I reacted so emotionally when I saw *Chorus Line* overseas. I know how those kids have suffered.

My next engagement was in the Fourth Kew Cubs when we performed a season of little playlets based on the Jungle books of Kipling. Absolutely no outsiders were permitted to see these ritualistic efforts. The drama unfolded behind locked doors, in the arcane glow of a Moon made from a circle of waxed paper and a light-globe. It was all very strange, but I suspect freemasons do much the same sort of thing at lodge meetings. Anyway, the cub mistress played Akela, Mowgli's friend, while various of us were cast as other animals. I'd wanted to be Shere Khan, the tiger, but David Preston got that part. Then I put up my hand to be Hathi, the wise elephant, but that went to John Sinclair. I don't remember what part I finally finished up with, but it was probably Winston the wombat or one of the Bandar-log monkey people. However, I quite enjoyed the bit where we all chanted: 'Dib, dib, dib,' — an acrostic for 'do our best.'

Oh, I shouldn't have told you that bit. It's forbidden – like revealing the Masonic handshake. Well, if I'm found choked to death with a Fourth Kew woggle you'll know what happened.

However, the years passed and no other parts were offered by adult management. So we amused ourselves by ad-libbing Batman and Robin episodes and in an endless round of Westerns in the playground. Pointing loaded fingers and going 'Ksh, ksh' with our mouths and dying magnificently, voluptuously. Stiffening as the bullet tore into our chests, toppling in slow motion, writhing and grimacing in our death throes. Then counting up to ten (well, five) before resurrecting ourselves for another exchange of fire.

Then, suddenly I was seventeen and working at the New Theatre in Melbourne as a part of my commitment to Bolshevism. No wonder Mr Menzies has been so intent on banning the Communist Party. There were about two dozen of us there, dangerous revolutionaries undermining capitalism by screening battered prints of *Battleship Potemkin* or staging productions of *Reedy River*.

The play in which I found myself was *The Merry Wives of Windsor*, a political polemic by William Shakespeare, the well-known Russian playwright. A farce involving a Sir John Falstaff, who keeps roaring things like: 'Let the sky rain potatoes! Let it thunder to the tune of *Greensleeves*'. It has parts for a number of comely matrons, a Welsh parson, a French doctor, a foolish country squire, an attractive soubrette and 'a well-born sensible young man and her persistent suitor'.

This latter role was foisted upon yours truly when the member of the Wharf Labourers' Union who'd won it in audition failed to turn up for the rehearsals. Apparently he'd been rostered on night shift. So I found myself in a pair of tights, a cod-piece made from one of those metal gussets worn by cricketers and a ruffled jacket complete with a heavy sword. And if the thought of Adams in tights fills you with disbelief I should point out that in the early Fifties I was living on five quid a week and was therefore comparatively slender.

David Niven has written a number of name-dropping, one-upping books about all the famous people he acted with in Hollywood. I don't wish to show him up, but our cast was far more glittering. For example, Falstaff was played by Bill Griffiths, whose wife was to become Senator Meltzer, while Mistress Quickly was played by a woman who achieved fame as Gerard Kennedy's Mum. As well, a young man in the cast turned up as a baddie in *Homicide,* while one of the merry wives appeared in a Trix commercial. It was, as you can see, a remarkable gathering of talent.

The play ran about three weeks, if 'ran' is the right word ('lurched' . . . 'staggered'). And many of the production problems emanated from me. First of all I'd forget the lines. Curiously, I could remember everybody else's. It was just my own that proved elusive. Second, I'd be out the back canoodling with the lady playing my beloved and would miss my cue. And, third, my sword, even when sheathed, turned out to be a most dangerous weapon. If I wasn't tripping over it, I'd turn suddenly so that it would strike someone an agonising blow on the shins. In the course of the first week most of my fellow performers were effectively crippled. Finally the enraged producer disarmed me and for the rest of the season I had to perform with a blunt paper knife stuck in my belt. Furthermore, I had to stand in a fixed position *vis-à-vis* the audience, such as it was, rather like an Egyptian bas relief. This was to conceal the prodigious ladder on the inside leg of my tights.

But the greatest catastrophe was to occur backstage. The girl playing Anna, my paramour, had just recently arrived from England trailing a husband remarkable for his jealously and tenacity of purpose. He used to hang around rehearsals looking murderous whenever Shakespeare required me to buss her cheek. And had he known what was going on backstage I'm sure he'd have run me through with my paper knife.

As often happens between romantic leads in stage productions – at least when they're of vaguely heterosexual persuasion – the romantic leads were drawn to one another. Thus we spent our off-stage moments in ardent embrace in a darkened passageway. This was to force the premature close of the season as, in a moment of romantic emphasis while giving her a particularly enthusiastic smooch, I pushed her backside through a pane of glass. Sadly the odd slither penetrated her charming posterior.

I suppose the word must have got around as it's taken almost twenty years to get another part. Even then, I could be accused of nepotism as I'm the film's producer. However, I must make it clear that I'm not 'doing a Hitchcock'. Far from seeking the role of Dr Pughson it was pressed upon me. I now suspect that Sheila Helpmann, Monica Maughan and Patricia Kennedy organised it in punishment for all the rotten things I said about them when I was a theatre critic. Either that, or they wanted me to learn, by direct experience, just what a debilitating business film acting can be, when you stand around for eight or ten hours to fill two or three minutes of screen time. If that *was* their plan they've won a convert, as I propose standing up at my next Equity meeting and supporting a move for a national strike. I know now that the glacial pace of film production is a crucifixion for the actor, particularly when there's somebody like me in the cast. Because I did it again. Just as I threw a spanner into the works of the East Kew school concert, just as I punctured the Merry Wives of Windsor. I wreaked havoc on *The Getting of Wisdom.*

The scene was enormously elaborate as Bruce Beresford was determined to do it in a single take. It shows Laura, our heroine, arriving for the first day of term and being snubbed by the group of girls who'd previously been her friends. In the same sequence there's an inordinate amount of peripheral detail, with the headmistress ticking off misbehaving children and inquiring about social goings-on from the older girls. As a porter carries luggage upstairs, Dr Pughson greets his fellow teachers and asks Laura whether she's persisted with her maths and all sorts of reunions take place. Finally, the girls are hurried upstairs by Mrs Gurley while we staff members gather in a small, self-important group.

It took hours to rehearse, to plot the movements of camera and cast, to choreograph the background action, to modulate the delivery. And what happened when we finally got around to a take? Everything went wonderfully until the very end when Dr Pughson joined his fellow teachers to watch the young ladies ascending Illawarra's splendid staircase. For, quite unconsciously, I did something that was quite in character for me but decidedly out of character for the maths master of the period. I put my arm around Mrs Gurley's waist and gave her bustled bum a friendly squeeze.

Bruce Beresford's cry of anguish will echo in my memory forever, along with the moans of the music teacher at the Kew town hall and the scream of the English actress as her bottom was quilled by pieces of that window.

It was as bad and as expensive a moment as any in the history of Australian cinema and recalls the great story about Cecil B de Mille filming the parting of the Red Sea, when five out of the six cameras malfunctioned at that million-dollar moment. Whereupon de Mille looked up to a nearby mountain top and called 'How about you?' to his most trusted associate, the operator of the final camera. And the operator replied: 'Ready when you are, CB.'

TV or not TV, that's a kwestion

SPOONER

Yu've properly red wear a profsa at univers-city says that wotchin tevelishun corses brane damij. And now the eggsactives at the telly chanel say that he's a ratbag corse it dussnt. Well, I don't wreckin it does ether. (Corse brane damij.) I wreckin telly is very good for the brane and teeches all sortsa use full things.

Four eggsample. Since wotchin *Sesamee Strete* four a mear for yeers I have lerned the alfabett write up to big k. Wots more, I no the numbas two. I can count rite up to twenny even when there not singin the song. As four sums, I am grate at adding up. Ask me what 2 and 2 make and I emmedi . . . imedi . . . bang my foot on the floor 3 times. Then theres otha things you can lern from otha shows. For eggsample, by wotchin Mister Godhelpus in *No. 96* you can lern to be delegate essen. And by wotchin *The Box* you can lern how to undo ladis bras.

And think of the things you get to no from wotchin cwiz shows. For eggsample, Bary Jones lerned how to be a member of parlment from been in *Pickabocks* with Bob and Doli Dyer. He also one a lot of prices like 10 years Omo and a trip to Disneland. And I'm tolled his garij is jamd to the rufe with menthoids and Violent Crumbles. I never miss wotchin *Celibrates Squars* myself witch is by Reg Grundy. I wreckin Reg Grundy has dunmore four educashun than all the scules and universe-cities put together course he has *thousands* of cwiz shows on.

And apart from gettin to no lotsa things from lissenin to the annsers, the show gives work to Logie-winners whove seen betta days, like Jimmy Hannn and that bloke that usta do the wistling for Cambridge ciggy ads. If it wasnt for Reg Grundy people like they and Tommy Hanln wood have nothin to look forward to eggsept dressing up as Humpfrey Bare.

(Incidentally, hav you ever wonderd whos in the Humpfrey Bareskin at the moment? It usta be Nole Ferryr but I'm tolled by a girl who dos the zodiak at *TV Weak* that its now Stewt Wagstiff.)

Anyway, I was saying how I like wotchin *Celibrates Squars* corse of all the celibates they have on it like Jimmy Hannn and Stewt Wagstiff and Uglidave Gray. They sit inside neon sines and tell fibs. Its eggsiting corse they all flash and you can win a garij full of Violent Crumbles.

Then theres the things you can lern by wotchin Hecta Crayfish shows like *Homoside* and *Divi 4,* starring Graham Kenedy's big brother Gerald. By wotchin those shows for a copula yeers I gotta no how to rob a bank, getting away with $3500 from the ANZ's Coburg branch last November. (I used the money to buy a garij full of Violent Crumbles as a hedge again stinflation.)

What otha use full skils hav I got from tevelishun? Well, I lernt to stick my crash helmet to the rufe with Supa-gloo 497 (you can lift your feet rite off the floor) and Ive lernt to sing bits out of 93 different songs in 30 seconds by lissening to the ads for Magicstick records.

And I can do a triffick imitashun of Ita Buttrose's lisp ('Thith weekth *Womenth Weekly* tellth how to turn scrapth from your dutht-bin into eggthiting catherolth'). And I can always gess witch mums got the Whirlpool. And you just never no wen things like that arnt goin to cum in use full.

I mean, imagin you were kidnaped by monsters like in *Loss In Space* and they sed they'd only let you go if you could gess witch mum had a Whirlpool or if you could sing 93 songs in 30 seconds. Or imagin you were traped in a sinking submarine like in Voyj to the Bottom of the See. By glooing your crash helmet to a girder and lifting your feet off the floor, you mite survive until Admiral Nelson thort up something clever.

Mind you, I dont like all the shows. I dont like the show in witch An Devason picks on people about their washin. Tork about the fivth degree. 'Are you *shore* they come out witer? Are you *certin*? Don't tel the viewers *lies*. Are you *positif*?' I wreckin thats an evashun of your privates. They should just give her their rank and serial numba like in *Mash* or *12 Aclock High.*

If the cops ever catch me for robin that ANZ bank I hope they dont get Devason to grill me in the back room. Corse Id confess even befour they had the globe shining in my eyes. Apart from anything else, shes even bigga than Margrit Witlam. Why dont they have someone nice do the Omo ads? Someone like Boo Boo Forkner. I wreckin An Devason ort to pick on people her own size, like in *World Champignon Ressling*.

So I dont wreckin that wotchin televishun corses brane damij at all. Look at me, I can dress myself and arnt wetting the bed nearly as offn. Mind you, Im not wot they call a heavy viewer at gist 12 hours a day. Nor have I been wotchin it all that long. Just since I gradjew . . . grad . . . left Oxfam Universe-city with my pee-h-dee in fizzics, having been ducks of Melbun Hi and a Roads scolar.

They're the family drawers

Today I wish to draw attention to the things commonly found in drawers. And before the Festival of Light starts mass-producing outraged letters in that characteristic crayon, let me stress that I'm referring to drawers found in chests and not to those worn below the waist. Not to knickers.

In every home in this nation you'll find a drawer or drawers devoted to the detritus of living, a place for objects of no practical use which, nonetheless, were considered too significant for the dustbin. Like the gloveboxes of cars (which contain everything but gloves) and women's handbags, such drawers become increasingly crowded and mysterious, as marvellous and instructive to explore as any Ming tomb. In a way, they're like family albums, except that they contain three-dimensional objects instead of photographs. So to sift through them with curious fingers is to re-trace your steps into the fungoid and forgotten past.

I've opened such a drawer in my desk to discover a staggering variety and quantity of defunct things. On a rough estimate, it contains approximately .05 per cent of Australia's gross national product. Yet I've no recollection of rescuing any of it. Perhaps it all just crawled in here to die. When those old cigarette lighters realised they were down to their last flint, perhaps they made their way here just as geriatric jumbos are alleged to seek secret burial grounds.

Anyway, let's have a quick inventory of my drawer's jetsam. For starters, there are about two dozen old keys for long-lost padlocks or the back doors of the homes I've left behind me. No point keeping any of them. Yet what civilised person could throw keys into a dustbin? There's too much innate dignity for that. Keys are like little crucifixes symbolising property instead of piety. Thus they accumulate in the darkness, or perhaps they fornicate. That'd account for all those little silver suitcase keys tangled in the paperclips.

And the paperclips. Someone has painstakingly linked them together into a six-foot chain. Did I do that? If so, why do I lose control on nights of a full moon? And here's a small photograph of Meyer Baba, one of the self-confessed gods of Indian origin who are currently luring our youth into wearing dhotis and eating brown rice. It was given to me by Adrian Rawlins, possibly Australia's most notable eccentric. Since I first met him at Yarra Park State School in the late Forties, Adrian has pursued fads as enthusiastically as a kelpie chasing cars, finally sinking his teeth into the Himalayan humbug. Still, he seems happy enough. When Adrian last paid me a visit he punctuated his conversation with little yelps. You'd have sworn he was sitting on a tack or a whoopee cushion. But he explained that his cries indicated rapture rather than rupture, being his response to feelings of inexpressible bliss.

Symbolising my sporting interests, the drawer divulges two dominoes and a marble. And there's a Masonic medal branded 'Nunawading Lodge No. 404, presented to the Worshipful Brother M B Burke on 11/4/45'. Well, old M B was my late and unlamented stepfather and that was the only medal he ever won, having escaped the dangers of World War Two by feigning everything from fallen arches to leprosy. (Come an army medical and he could produce symptoms for which there were no known disease.) I can still see him going off to lodge meetings.in his funny apron as though on his way to some arcane barbecue, undoubtedly involving blood sacrifice.

Then there's a variety of political memorabilia, such as a balloon bearing a portrait of Lyndon Johnson. As you blow it up, the President's head swells to alarming, ten-gallon proportions appropriate to his Texan origins and his epic ego. Such balloons were handed out by officials to the crowds that lined the route of his Second Coming to this country, a visit designed to ensure the re-election of Harold 'All the Way' Holt. I've also got a poignant 'It's Time' badge and one reading 'Impeach Nixon', whoever he was.

This brings me to a knob of grey plasticine – at least I hope it's grey plasticine – and to a piece of quartz on which has been inscribed 'this tooth belonged to Barry Broadbent'. And there's a sort of Lone Ranger mask minus the eyeholes that Qantas gave me when I couldn't stand their inflight movie. Plus there's a split golfball, a china door knob and a wooden puzzle from Japan – according to the accompanying piece of rice paper, 'any skilful person can reassemble in two minutes'. Always provided that you can disassemble the wretched thing. I never could, finding it as inviolable as Fort Knox.

There's also some book matches from Rome's Cavalieri Hilton, the only place I could bribe my way into during a hotel-employees' strike. I remember it vividly because you had to cook your own pasta in the kitchen and make your own beds. Yet the management didn't hesitate to hit me for fifteen per cent service charge. Another thing that made the stay memorable was the way the staff would crowd outside every morning at six o'clock to bang dustbins together, thus producing the loudest noise since the detonation of Krakatoa. Still it saved ringing reception for one of those early morning calls they invariably forget. And the book matches conjure another image. Half-owned by the Vatican, the Hilton was frequented by Fellini-esque cardinals who'd roll up in their Bentleys and technicolour drag (they looked like embroidered cushions) with chauffeurs who were dead ringers for Valentino or Vic Damone. Ah, *la dolce vita.*

There are also two pairs of sunglasses minus one or the other lens. I suppose these were kept in case any one-eyed beggar presented himself squinting in the doorway. There are also three of those spring-loaded tapes that measure things in anachronistic and illegal inches. So there's every chance we'll have a midnight visit from the metric Gestapo. (I'm told you get three months for possessing a foot ruler and a year if your milk's in pint bottles.) Then there's a packet of five-hundred Wasp air-gun pellets which I use to shoot spooky black caterpillars. Although I've an almost Buddhist reverence for life that extends even to ants and Young Liberals, I loathe those grubs. They defoliate my gum trees as effectively as the Pentagon did Vietnam. Impervious to spraying (in that they're too high to reach) and closely resembling Sir Robert Menzies' eyebrows, they cluster together forming fur collars on the uppermost branches. So I put on a solar topee and, with the help of my native bearers and loaders, shoot the buggers. Of course, it's one thing to talk to the trees and quite another to be seen apparently attempting to assassinate them. Which may explain why the neighbours are taking up a petition to have me committed.

Then there's a genuine historical document: namely a receipt for a four-shilling donation to the Federal Labor Party's Campaign Fund signed, in pencil, by J B Chifley as Prime Minister. In the age of Watergate, of million dollar TV campaigns and secret slush funds, I find that torn piece of paper very endearing.

What else? There's the solitary Butter Menthol covered in fluff and three nondescript pieces of rock souvenired by a larrikin cobber from the Forum, the Pyramids and Pompeii. But apart from provoking tut-tuts at such okerology, they're precious little magic for me because I have no idea which is which. And I could mention the three broken watches which (Uri Geller please note) invariably start ticking for a few minutes whenever they're disturbed from their ancient slumbers. But enough is enough. Instead let me urge you to delve and lucky dip in your own drawers. It's as much fun as holding a seance or diving on an old wreck.

Indeed, I'm sure the agonising process of psycho-analysis would be short-circuited (cut back from twenty years to twenty minutes) if only we'd empty our drawers on our shrink's desk. Take Malcolm Fraser's drawers as an example. (Let there be no question of bias here – I chose him entirely at random.) If he was to show the contents at his next appointment, his psychiatrist would find it easy to drawer the right conclusion. Quite apart from the fluffy Butter Menthol and the Lyndon Johnson balloon I'm sure we've got in common, Mal's top-drawer would contain keys to inner-most beings, clues as significant as Citizen Kane's Rosebud. Things like his scout's woggle and his prefect's badge and the Batman comics he confiscated from his fag.

Of Anzacs and Aztecs

**Ockers abroad
as the fount
of civilisation**

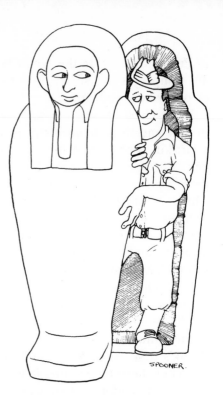

SPOONER.

Giant rock carvings resembling some made in ancient Egypt have been found in mountain country north of Proserpine in northern Queensland.

The carvings were found by a young grazier, Mr Ron Muller, last weekend in the Drayander Ranges.

They had been sighted in 1936 by a party of four orchid hunters who could not give an accurate description of the location.

The find adds weight to a theory that Australia was visited by ancient Egyptians which has been promoted by Dr Rex Gillroy, curator of the Natural History Museum at Mt Victoria in New South Wales.

For some time Dr Gillroy has claimed eucalyptus oil and what appeared to be a mummified kangaroo were found in the tomb of an ancient king in the Nile Valley.

– Recent report in the Australian Press

You don't have to be Margaret Daniken or Eric Von Mead to observe eerie links between Ancient Egypt and Australia. Look at the popularity here of Nile handkerchiefs, Camel T-shirts, Cleo magazine and Patra orange juice. Open the yellow pages and the pigmented papyrus discloses Pyramid Paper Products and the Pharoah's Massage Parlour. And who has stood outside the fibro RSL Hall in Carnegie and not been reminded of the great temples of Karnak? (Carnegie, Karnak – the link is obvious.)

Then there is the striking similarity between the chariots driven by the Egyptian generals in their wars against the Libyans, and the Model Dairy milk carts. Not to mention the way both your Ancient Wogs and your Australians love their beer (or pior as the Gippos called it). And consider the way many a faded wallpaper has depicted glittering occasions at the Royal Palace at Thebes, where the men and women stood at opposite ends of the room.

Fascinated, I've been digging deeper, hoping to find other examples of cultural influence from that enigmatic civilisation that sprang up on the flood plains of the Nile some 5000 years ago. And within weeks I'd found that ancient Egyptian medicine was being practised in most of our suburbs. A manipulative technique despised by the AMA, it's known as Chiro (i.e. Cairo) practice. I've been haunted by the thought of that mummified kangaroo dying in climes, as alien as Hemingway's frozen leopard on Mt Kilimanjaro. Thus people would find me shining my torch on the hieroglyphs in our tomb-like public loos. Or I'd be seen standing in a trance on the banks of the Yarra, imagining the discovery of baby Moses in the bullrushes where, in fact, I'd be staring at a drowned cat.

Then, a few weeks back, I got my breakthrough. What if everyone was approaching the subject from the wrong angle? What if Australia *hadn't* been visited by Egyptians? What if Egyptian civilisation had been founded by *Australians?*

You may well laugh. Just as people laughed at Galilei Galileo, at Christopher Columbus, at William McMahon. But within hours my hypothesis was being validated by a rush of evidence. After all, is it likely that a group of wogs in the Middle East had suffcient brains to give the world the calendar, the alphabet and beer? Isn't it more likely that we Anzacs got the ball rolling? You've only to cast a phrenologist's eye over Ayers Rock to know that ours is a landscape surging with creativity.

There was no doubt in my mind. It was *our* forebears, filled with Australia's pioneering spirit, who exported civilisation to the four corners of the globe. After all, you see an echo of the same determination as our grandmas rocket about on the *Women's Weekly* World Discovery Tour.

The jigsaw fell into place when I contemplated Australia's major pyramid, Melbourne's Shrine of Remembrance. Just as the great pyramids were built within easy reach of the Nile, this mighty and mysterious edifice was constructed by the ancient Anzacs within a few hundred yards of the Yarra. And such was the Anzacs' zeal for construction that they built thousands of equally enigmatic structures, in stone and concrete, throughout this vast nation. Frequently in the form of what's popularly called a Cleopatra's Needle, you find them outside town halls and in parks or in the middle of shopping centres. (For example, a very fine example, complete with ineptly carved sphinxes, can be observed diagonally opposite David Jones in Sydney.) And because of faulty scholarship, these enigmatic structures have been mislabelled War Memorials when they are, in fact, symbols of the Anzacs' complex theology.

Meanwhile, across the Pacific, all but identical structures to the Shrine of Remembrance can be seen rising from the Mexican plains or rearing above the Paraguayan jungles. Great, crumbling pyramids that, like the Melbourne example, contain dank tunnels and echoing chambers. Can this be mere coincidence? It is my conviction that these too were built by the Anzacs who, somehow, had reached South America in distant times. Indeed, it's palpably obvious that the name Anzac underwent subtle changes, becoming Aztec with the passage of time.

Again and again I turned my attention to the limpid waters of the Yarra, where the paddle steamer from Princes Bridge has plied since time immemorial. And I remembered my school teachers telling me that name Yarra was Abo for something. Like hell it was! Suddenly I heard my ancient Anzacs chanting to the Sun God, to Ra, the same deity that stands triumphantly atop the Egyptians' hierarchy of gods. 'Yea, Ra,' they cried, as his rays filtered through the red gums, illuminating the adoring faces of citizens called Wocker, Slob-guts and Bluey. Thus Yea-Ra became Yarra, the most beloved tributary in this land of Sun-worshippers.

But how you ask, did the ancient Anzacs reach the South Americas? How did they sail the vast distances to the Suez Canal all those thousands upon thousands of years ago? Here I introduce evidence provided by colleague Thor Heyerdahl whose epic journeys on the Kon Tiki rafts and by papyrus boat demonstrated the possibility of intercontinental travel in the centuries before P & O.

'In my opinion and in my interesting Dutch accent, rowing eights from the boatsheds along the Yarra, carrying crews from Melbourne's public schools, could have reached those distant countries. It could have happened very simply. Perhaps they were blown off course during Henley on the Yea-Ra or during the Head of the River on the Barwon. Or perhaps the cox made an error in navigation.'

Admittedly some of the evidence is circumstantial. For example, I cannot place much weight on the remarkable facial similarities between Bob Hawke and Horus, the falcon-headed god. Nor can I place too much significance on the way the Egyptians deified a wide variety of animals and birds, just as today's Anzacs cheer the Kangas, the Swans and the Magpies. But I believe any fair-minded person would have to acknowledge that, on balance, my theory seems the likeliest explanation. Thus the Melbourne depicted in Stanley Kramer's *On the Beach* as the grave of civilisation ('I couldn't think of a better place,' said Ava Gardner) was also the one true cradle. Sorry about that, Bahrain and Babylon, not to mention Brisbane and Launceston.

Of course, conventional historians will ridicule me, because of their absurd commitment to a ludicrously inaccurate history which was Captain Cook arriving here but ten minutes ago. Whereas my theory places the white man in this country a good 500,000 years previously. (I believe that Aboriginals are the descendants of these original whites who, inevitably, have suffered seriously from sunburn.) And I'll go further. I'm convinced that most of the world was founded by voyaging Australians. Look at the Vikings whose drunkenness, raping and pillaging is perfectly in accord with the conduct of young Australians travelling overseas today. As it happens, I wouldn't be at all surprised if those so-called Viking galleons were really rowing eights from Geelong Grammar. Come to think of it, the word Viking (or something very like it) is constantly employed as an adjective in our colloquial conversation. It's viking this, viking that, all the viking time.

However, I have had one serious difficulty. For I could find no tradition of mummification within Anzac society. However, I'm pleased to announce a major archaeological find as a result of a dig at the ·Paris end of Collins Street. Having finally broken through the sealed portal to the Melbourne Club, my associates were confronted by a remarkable sight. Behind a warp and weft of cobweb, they saw a great many men who'd been leaders in Australian politics and commerce. And with a few sad exceptions, they were all in a remarkable state of preservation.

Around the world in eighty unzips

As I've just returned from eight weeks in foreign parts with my attitudes as provincial and prejudiced as ever, I cannot agree that travel broadens the mind. However, there can be no doubt that it places an enormous strain on the bladder. With painful memories of searching London for a loo, Ireland for a bog and the Netherlands for a dyke, I have to report that they're as rare as oases in the Gobi. Every now and then something promising would swim into view, but it would turn out to be a mirage or a public telephone. Such was my plight in Denmark that at Elsinore Castle I was sorely tempted to use an unoccupied sentry box.

Since the collapse of the last Roman aquaduct, plumbing facilities have become a thing of the past in Italy, so that the only public WC to be found is the famous six-holer in Pompeii. And you can't get near that for Americans with Instamatics. So you waddle around Florence and Pisa with your legs crossed while the liquid thoroughfares of Venice mock and intensify your agony.

Given the atrocious plumbing in Paris (where the Clochemerle-style urinal has fallen victim to social progress and where everyone makes matters worse by saying *Oui* all the time), it's easy to understand why my fellow-travelling Prime Minister cuts short his overseas trips. He comes back to visit the men's room.

Tourists are notorious for rushing through the Louvre and the Uffizi as though attempting the four-minute mile. This is usually attributed to their crassness and Philistinism, but the truth is simply that they're bursting and can't find the relief they seek.

On balance, Rome is the worst of cities, as around every corner just where you'd expect a public loo, there's another bloody fountain. And one's urinary tract is very suggestible. Thus just as a camel is forced by its harsh environment to go weeks without drinking water, the traveller is forced to go days without passing it. This is worst of all in winter's sub-zero temperatures. So I recommend when visiting your doctor for your shots, you have him perform a quick colostomy, whereby a disposable bag is fitted to your nether portions. Otherwise throughout your trip you'll be forced into restaurants to order meals you don't want just so you can lurch out the back. Even then – when seconds count – you're likely to open the wrong door and burst into the kitchen or the broom cupboard.

As well as being hard to find, foreign facilities are very alien to the Australian experience. Some lavs have stereophonic bowls, the one on the left being a bidet (French for footbath), while others have no bowls at all. Throughout Japan and Italy, for example, there are just ceramic craters, so that a normally serene and restful experience requires a considerable degree of courage and athleticism.

Even stranger is the nomenclature, which seems to be deliberately misleading. Thus one's lady wife, in her hour of need in Munich, is confronted by a door emblazoned with HERR when what the Nazi swine really mean is HIS.

In the hope of helping those of you who wish to spend a penny, centime or zloty on some forthcoming junket, let me give you the drum. Please read these paragraphs carefully as you'll be asked questions afterwards.

In civilised countries like Australia, the facilities are usually known as 'toilets', with the first syllable deriving from a symptom of constipation. Alternatively, they're 'lavatories', where the first two syllables, appropriately enough, suggest a sort of volcanic activity. Then there's our colloquial term 'dunny', so evocative of the sunburnt landscape.

In contrast, the Americans prefer such charming euphemisms as 'powder room', which is perfectly appropriate to both sexes when you consider the tendency of the American male to use a wide range of cosmetics. The Europeans confuse the issue by calling their facilities ridiculous things like 'retretes', 'elvaters', 'servicios', 'aborts', 'gabinettos', 'casa de banhos', 'klozets', 'nuzniks' and 'zahods'. As a result, you can expire while desperately turning the pages of your Nicaraguan or Yugoslavian phrasebook.

Then comes the question of differentiating between the sexes. In our country, doors are clearly marked Gents and Ladies, His and Hers, Men and Women, while in American hotel they can be Squaws and Braves or Guys and Dolls. All of which are perfectly clear.

But in Norway the doors read Herrer for men and Kvinner for women, while the Yugoslavs have a variety of terms, including Gospode, Zene, Zenske, Gospodin, Muski and Muskarci. Consequently, you don't know whether you're Arthur or Martha. As for the Italians, they confuse the issue with Signore and Signori, quite indistinguishable when you're in a hurry, or Donne and Uomini, which are perplexing even at one's leisure. The Austrians go for the mysterious Frauern and Manner, while the Portugese are Senhoras and Homens. And what red-blooded Australian man could enter a door with *that* on it? I prefer the Spanish Caballeros or Hombres, which are more suggestive of virility.

Then there's a tendency to use inexplicable, multi-national symbols. In most airport terminals the loos are identified with little circles with arrows protruding from them, either up or down. And these manage to be at once suggestive and incomprehensible, turning a trip to the loo into a form of roulette. The variation on this is the use of silhouettes, where one door shows a person in trousers while the other depicts someone in a skirt. Yet even this poses problems in cities like Athens and Edinburgh, where many of the military wear kilts, or in the USA where the women wear the trousers.

Not that it really matters which dunny you go into in Europe, as every male toilet has a woman sitting inside the door who scrutinises you both coming and going, not to mention during. This is to bully you into leaving a few francs, kroner or kopeks in her saucer. But in most cases I found the experience so unnerving that I was immediately afflicted with a stricture and couldn't get my money's worth. Thank God we've higher moral standards in this country.

A few days ago I found myself standing outside the orang-outang enclosure in Dublin Zoo. There were no bars between us, only a moat. And as I stood studying the facial expressions of this sizable simian, so reminiscent of Brendan Behan and other Irish intellectuals, it started to behave in an extremely aggressive manner. For he began throwing his collection of dried nodules of dung at me. What's more, he did so with unerring accuracy.

Thinking back, I see that as symbolic. It perfectly expresses the European attitude towards the tourist, once they've lured you into their clutches with their travel posters.

Record-breaking among the ruins

Australia is fortunate in that it combines a lot of geography with very little history. If we ignore the ancient culture of the Aborigines, which most of us do, everything began just 200 years back with the first Cook's tour. This means we're mercifully free of antique monuments, old cathedrals and 15th century ruins while being richly blessed with high-rise office buildings and display homes.

I'm inclined to agree with a writer friend of mine, of European extraction, who says that our cities have the impermanent look of film sets. In contrast Europe groans beneath the weight of history and their entire landscape is littered with crumbling edifices. But instead of being ashamed of these decrepit buildings, these perverse Europeans seem fond of them. Moreover they expect foreigners to inspect them and are enormously insulted if you don't squander money on guides, guide books and sets of slides.

Now, every Australian knows that overseas travel has just one real purpose. *Duty free shopping.* And it's enormously encouraging to see more and more of us queueing up at customs at Mascot and Tullamarine with our cartons full of trannies and Johnny Walker bought at a useful discount in Singapore. This shows our growing sophistication and our ability to come to terms with our Asian destiny.

However, from time to time you'll find it impossible to avoid such boring, ramshackle places as Florence and

Venice as they tend to be included in the budget-priced package tours. Apart from the fact that duty-free shops are even harder to find than public toilets in these Italian slums, local custom demands that you feign interest in their architectural flotsam.

Now, an experienced traveller can waste a great deal of time in such places which could be better invested in buying lurid knick-knacks. Take Florence where you'll be required to plod around a draughty old dump called the Ufizzi which is full of murky old religious paintings. Hardly a nuddy in the place. Fortunately a lot of Florence's art treasures were destroyed in a catastrophic flood, and more of them are going to rack and ruin because of the lack of funds for their conservation. (This is an excellent policy on behalf of the central government, as within a few years most of Italy's ruins will be in ruins and all those acres of Botticellis and Titians will have disintegrated from neglect.)

Nonetheless you'll be expected to trudge around the leftovers. But the whole tedious business can be curtailed if you follow the lead of the Australians who've gone before you. Because we Aussies are without doubt the world's fastest tourists. For example, a bus load of middle-aged ladies on a *Women's Weekly* World Discovery Tour hold the record for the Louvre: just 4 minutes 58 seconds. This amazing figure was recorded on a windless day in November of '72 from a standing start by a Winged Victory. The ladies rushed through the Egyptian sculptors, past the Watteaus and Fragonards, rounding the Mona Lisa in ninety seconds flat. They then sprinted through the Impressionists, pausing for customary ten seconds by the Van Goghs and Lautrecs, and made it back to the bus in time to shave two seconds off the previous record established in 1971 by a package-tour of Wisconsin widows.

It is with this brave spirit that one must confront the shambles that is Renaissance Italy, where the ravages of time and war have done a job worthy of our own admirable Whelan. Take my own efforts a few days back in Florence. On arrival at the hotel I invested 850 lira in a little book entitled *How to See Florence in Two Days* and by studying the maps carefully was able to do the Medici Tombs, the Palazzo Pitti and the Ponte Vecchio in just over thirty minutes. Then there was my spirited attempt on the existing world record for a complete circuit of the Baptistry, including a mandatory glance at Ghiberti's frowzy old doors. (It's about time somebody took to them with the Brasso.) My best time was ninety-four seconds but the umpires refused to count it as a record because of slight wind assistance. As well, I was speeded on my way by the various deposits left by dogs on the cobbled square. (Dogs besmirch almost all of Europe's pavements, particularly in Florence and London, and as such pose a constant threat to the unwary. However, the experienced tourist turns them to his advantage by virtually skating around the so-called points of interest.)

I didn't do so well on my attempt on the Medici tombs record as a couple of sculptures caught my eye. And if you really want to cover ground, you must not become interested in any of the art works or architectural details. Instead you must stare resolutely ahead, turning a blind eye to whatever is being displayed whether they're the adenoids of St George preserved in some diamond-encrusted reliquary, or some painting purporting to be a Leonardo.

This is made easier by the Australian's natural indifference to beauty and by the suspicion that most of the exhibits are fake. For example, the Florentines claim to have the original of Michelangelo's David when everyone in Australia knows that it belongs to David Jones. Or is it Myers? I distinctly remember the Vice Squad raid.

As for the piece of the One True Cross you see in various cathedrals, if you put them all together you'd have enough wood to lay sleepers across the Nullarbor. (And there are other insults to the tourist's intelligence. Pisa's only claim to fame is a laughable piece of jerry-building, while in Paris you're supposed to be enthralled by the Eiffel Tower when after a hundred years all they've managed to do is put up the framework. And in one of the major Florence galleries they've got the cheek to display a collection of Michelangelo's statues that aren't even finished.)

In any event, the trick in such places is to keep your eyes slightly out of focus so that it all passes in a painless blur. But please, no short cuts. It is essential that you actually *pass* all the works considered masterpieces, just as you're required to pass the check-points in a car rally.

As a contrast to the backward places like Venice and Florence, Rome has a couple of quite reasonable shopping centres with Colonel Sanders outlets and Wimpy Bars. Moreover, the pace of this city's traffic enables you to rush around the monuments without looking conspicuous. Nor do you need to look to the left or right when crossing the road as all the cars in Italy are tiny little Fiats which are incapable of injuring a pedestrian. (Instead of fining Fiats for traffic infractions, the police simply squirt them with Mortein.) So by throwing yourself into the fray you should be able to knock off the Colosseum, the Forum and St Peter's in plenty of time for morning tea. Or capuccino, as we of the *cognoscenti* call it.

Incidentally, at the moment there's an alarming shortage of coins in Italy, so one often gets change in the form of matches or chocolates or packets of toothpicks. As a result it is now quite respectable to put buttons in the collection plate. But as you'll appreciate, it makes throwing coins in the Trevi fountain impossible. However, the Italian tourist officials have a man on duty who takes Diners Club.

While Australians are pre-eminent in high-speed touring and will certainly pick up most of the gold medals when it becomes an Olympic event, I predict a strong challenge from the ubiquitous Japanese. Despite their short legs, Japanese tourists can really cover some ground. I suppose they're able to practise by rushing about in Tokyo's vast railway stations. Be that as it may, I really had my work cut out keeping ahead of them in the Doge's Palace. But in the run to the altar rail in St Mark's, I won in a photo finish.

102

It's time for an old bookworm to turn

It's the time of year when reporters are doing the ring-arounds. They'll say it's Harry Knackers of the *Bugle* or Fiona Breakspear of *Ladies' Own* and ask you what you want for Christmas, what was your favourite Christmas, what you'd like for Christmas dinner or what will be your New Year's resolution. And you grit your teeth and extrude a witless witticism to help them pad their page. But this call is different. It's a bloke from the *Sun* who wants to know 'what interesting books have you read this year?'

Thoughts wheel around the head like galahs frightened from a dead gum. Obviously I must reel off a dozen impressive, esoteric titles to demonstrate my erudition, scholarship

103

and refined sensibility. I'm tempted to ask the bloke what titles Max Harris gave, so as to be sure of one-upping him. During the time it takes me to say 'ummm ... ' I decide to opt for an eclectic collection of authors ranging from Dostoyevsky (he's always safe) to Saul what's-his-name who won the Nobel Prize. Or is he too ordinary? Would people think that I was old hat?

In any case, what if the *Sun* bloke asks me the title? Then I'd be in big trouble, not having read a word of Saul what's-his-name's. Patrick White sounds a bit *passé* and for all I know Nabokov's dead. And Luis Borges was so 'in' a few years back he's probably out by now, along with Kurt Vonnegut. In any case, I did leaf through a Vonnegut a few years back and was very unimpressed. It read like talk balloons in search of a comic. And perhaps I shouldn't admit to reading novels at all. What if they were *de trop?* Perhaps sociology and economics are the go these days, and I should toss off a name like Chomsky, whoever he is.

'Who else have you asked?' I say, stalling for time. After all, if this is the showbiz list with people like Mike Willesee and Graham Kennedy, they'll be opting for easy books like *All The President's Men* or *The Noël Coward Story*. On the other hand, it could be like last year with me low man on the totem with Don Dunstan and Donald Horne – who'd blast me out of the water with writers like Geoffrey Barraclough and Robert Craft, whoever they are. In any event, shouldn't I name a female author, like Evelyn Waugh, just so I won't sound chauvinistic? Or was feminism last year?

Whereupon something extraordinary happens, I find myself blurting out the truth. That I haven't read anything, except for David Niven's latest, which I started reading on the last leg of my last trip with Qantas and pinched from their little library so that I could finish it later. Which I didn't. Mind you, I go on to explain that I buy books all the time. Continually. About a dozen a week. That as far as I'm concerned, buying books is of religious significance, an act of intellectual penance. Indeed, to turn the pages of a book is tantamount to spinning a prayer wheel or to telling one's beads. To open a book, that is a hard-cover book, is like opening the Koran or the Old Testament. So I buy books. And I open them. It's just that I don't *read* them any more.

As I explain to the man from the *Sun,* the house is full of books. I'm not one of those *poseurs* who go for showy, coffee-table volumes. I plonk books *everywhere.* On the floor in front of the telly (who do I think I'm kidding?) and on the chairs and mantelpiece. I even rumple the cover so they look used and loved. And from time to time, when they've sat around the room long enough, I take them to the library and squeeze them on to the long-choked shelves. With the other books I haven't read either. I even take the time to organise them by subject, by author, by alphabet. Although I do prefer to arrange them on the shelves according to their appearance, to their height and to the colour of their spines. I mean, you don't want too many dark books together or too many light ones. So I shift them around in a sort of literary impressionism.

The *Sun* bloke is thinking I'm mad, so I explain it's not really a waste of money to buy books that remain unread. Think of all the wealthy used-car dealers, who buy paintings they don't look at. In any case, books have a strange, mystical quality. They radiate wisdom like those Shell strips radiate insecticide. Which is why one feels awed and spiritual in the libraries, while even the most ignorant yobboes whisper in the presence of books. I believe that just to be *near* them is uplifting and nourishing, that you can almost absorb their contents by osmosis.

I tell the reporter a story about Bismarck. When he wanted a little rest from blood, sweat and tears he used to go out into his garden and hug a tree. In a way books are like trees. After all, they're made from trees. So just to cart books around is good for you. After all, Bismarck didn't actually *climb* trees. A warm embrace was more than adequate. And I do more than hug books. I pay for them, open them, turn a few pages, even smell them. I commune with books the way Wordsworth did with daffodils.

Yes, books to me are a sort of faith. And how many Christians read the Bible? For it's one thing to profess a religion and another to practise it. I must confess that my formal observances have taken something of a nosedive, that I've yielded to the temptations of the telly, to the promiscuous appeals of the magazine, to the seductions of the cinema.

Yet it wasn't always so. As a little boy I read my way through the Kew library in about two years flat. They couldn't buy them fast enough. My grandparents would say: 'Stop reading all the time – it isn't healthy. Go outside and play.' But I turned a deaf ear and continued ploughing through Richmal Crompton, Enid Blyton, Captain W E Johns, Edgar Rice Burroughs, and Mary Grant Bruce. The pejorative of bookworm was applied to me by everyone, and the thought of books being unhealthy was emphasised every time I visited the library. For I'd see half a dozen titles locked away inside the librarian's steriliser.

I was later to realise that these books were being quarantined, lest they spread measles or polio. But for me books had a contagion all their own, so that I entered my teenage years hopelessly afflicted and addicted. If I wasn't reading I felt sharp withdrawal symptoms, a strong anxiety. It was easy to read down in the loo because of the torn newspapers Gran hung on the nail.

It was easy to read at the meal table, because Grandpa used to fold his newspaper and prop it on the sauce bottle, a practice that has made me adept at reading upside down. And if I exhausted the text, there was always the label on the bottle itself. Mind you, the Worcestershire sauce labels were better reading than White Crow tomato. Lots of fine print about the traditional recipe of herbs and spices and about the suitability of the sauce for all forms of meat, including fish and fowl. The bathroom was a problem, as the literary possibilities of a toothpaste tube were easily exhausted.

Later on I began to read Tolstoy and Steinbeck and Waugh and Hemingway and Faulkner with the same rapacious appetite. I'd read five, six, ten books a week with a desperate sense of keeping up, of the need to absorb thousands of years of writing while still the authors were writing more. I became a high-speed reader long before it became a vogue, my eyes racing ahead of my brain, my ability to comprehend and absorb. Now it *was* unhealthy. Completely obsessive. Yet, twenty years later, I'm frequently astonished by the way an image from one of those novels will suddenly appear in my mind, vivid and compelling.

I explain to the man from the *Sun* that, these days, I fast-read magazines, still feeling the need to keep abreast of things, looking for thought-starters for columns. In a sense, magazines have been my methadone treatment, my substitute for the hard-stuff of hard covers. Yet such reading is strangely unsatisfying, proving that mind cannot live by magazine alone. For someone like me, a magazine is about as satisfying as lemonade to a dipso. Not even paperbacks are much use. They feel too trivial, too disposable. They lack the solidity of proper books, their *gravitas*. They are to literature what the Kleenex tissue is to the hankie.

There's even something repellent about the paper in a magazine. The eyes slide and slither over all that gloss. And just as you feel hungry half an hour after a Chinese meal, magazines leave the hollow feeling in the mind. Whereas the eye comes to grips with the fluffy surface of book paper. The magazine, like the TV show, is ephemera where the book has substance, weight. A book requires a commitment. It is a collaboration between you and the writer. You set your own pace, your own rhythms, rushing here, dawdling there, turning back to retrace some steps. You have to imagine the faces, the places, the decor, the lighting. Imagine you're reading *War and Peace.* Your Natasha becomes a fusion, a synthesis of romantic ideals that no Audrey Hepburn or whoever could possibly challenge. And that's the problem with the new media of film and television. They do the imagining for you, and all too often their imagination is pedestrian.

I've always longed to write books, real books, with hard covers. Books that get cards in library indexes. Even if nobody read them after a year or so, they'd still be there. Whereas to write on newsprint is as insubstantial as writing on the wind. It's forgotten before it's read and used to wrap the rubbish. In these days of Lady Scott prints and pastels, you don't even have a second chance to be noticed on that nail in the sentry box. It's like being a pavement artist and seeing your work first smudged and then erased by the shoes of the crowd.

Yet whenever I've been asked to write a book by this or that publisher, I decline. There's no point in trying. I can't write more than a thousand words on anything. After years of working to a deadline and a space, the thousand-and-first word fails me. It doesn't matter if I'm writing about a trip to the supermarket or the history of Western civilisation. At 900 words I'm going, going. And at a thousand and one, I'm gone. Something written for a newspaper lives a single day. And film making is scarcely more satisfying as it's too much a social art, too impersonal. But a book is something one does alone, in splendid isolation.

Which is why, as a child, I believed writers to be gods. In the 1950s there was a chance I'd get to meet Steinbeck, and I remember feeling as nervous and as weak-kneed as a pre-pubescent schoolgirl about to see a Bay City Roller. Yet now, though words gush from my typewriter like water from a broken hydrant, millions of words over the years, the novel continues to mock me. To ask me to write a book is as hopeless as asking a tap-dancer to run a marathon.

Perhaps that's one of the reasons I've stopped reading

108

novels. Yet I must have kept every one I read for twenty years. Camus, Sartre, Ralph Ellison. And, as surely as bricks build buildings, books build consciousness. But when I bring new books to the sizeable collection, Camus, Sartre and Ellison know that I'm a fraud.

Some people use books to prop up a wobbly table. I use them to prop a wobbly mind. As Anthony Burgess said (not that I've read his books – but I did see a couple of his movies): 'The possession of a book becomes a substitute for reading it.' Some books, said Francis Bacon, are to be tasted. Others are to be sampled and a few to be digested. I sip at them like a wine-bibber, rolling paragraphs around the mind, to assess their flavour, their bouquet, their 'nose'. Or rather, their 'brow'. I do this by picking a book from the shelves on my way to the loo. But I never pick the same book twice, so that in the course of a week a letter of Evelyn Waugh's merges with a political observation by Gary Wills to become a joke by Wodehouse and a memory of Hal Porter's. I'm worse than someone who reads those condensed books or who reads nothing but reviews. The procedure turns literature into a sort of confetti.

Thus has this bookworm turned. God knows what the bloke from the *Sun* made of my confession. I suppose they'll print a couple of words out of context. What I do know is that I'll be making a New Year's resolution to turn the telly to the wall, to cancel all those irrelevant subscriptions, to start really reading again. But if there's one thing more evanescent than a newspaper column it's a New Year's resolution.

'A dog's nose
and a maid's knees
are always cold'

Animals have these advantages over man. They never hear the clock strike. They die without any idea of death. They have no theologians to instruct them. Their last moments are not disturbed by unwelcome and unpleasant ceremonies. Their funerals cost them nothing, and no-one starts law suits over their wills.

Voltaire in a letter to
Count de Schomberg, 1769

What astonished him was that cats should have two holes cut in their coats exactly at the places where their eyes were.

G C Licthenberg, 1779

I'd make a rotten St Francis. Apart from the technical difficulty of not being a 13th century Catholic, I don't get on with animals. Indeed, my track record with fauna boggles the mind. Come to think of it, I'd make an even worse Johnny Weismuller. In those early Tarzan films, he'd only to beat his pectorals and yodel to bring half Africa loppoping to his feet. Elephants, ostriches, rhinocerae, the lot.

In contrast, I've only to approach a bird cage for the budgie to hurl itself from the perch and crash lifeless on the shell-grit below. No matter how engagingly I simper 'here pussy', cats slink from my path or throw themselves beneath the wheels of passing cars. Dogs yelp at my friendly overtures and horses roll on their backs and stick their legs in the air. It was always thus. As a child, my guinea pigs cashed in their chips. My lizards languished. Yabbies scorned my baited string. My tadpoles turned their toes up. My white mice ate each other. At the sound of my foot fall, my pet tortoise would take off like a GTHO Falcon. I even gave warts to my frogs.

In recent years, I did have one dog that seemed to like me. Or perhaps it was toleration. I bought it as a puppy from an urchin who came to the door claiming it to be a pedigreed Australian terrier. However, it soon grew into a monstrous mastiff, a bitzer showing unmistakable traces of Siberian wolf-hound, not to mention Alaskan malamute. It was no trouble to feed; you just tossed it unopened cans. And as if to express its affection, it only savaged me on three occasions, choosing to vent its spleen on tradesmen and passing children.

Almost every day I'd find another grisly token in the driveway. A chewed mail bag, a bloodied wallet, a mauled exercise book, a gnawed spoke from the milk cart. Worse still, the brute would excavate vast holes in the garden, so as to accommodate its ghastly collection of extremely large bones. Finally the neighbours marched on me at night. I can still see their angry faces illuminated by burning torches and hear the sounds of shouting voices as bricks smashed through my windows. So there was nothing for it but send Tich (we'd named him during his terrier stage) away to a farm in the country. Someone once defined the dog as the only animal who has seen his God. If so, one couldn't blame Tich for turning agnostic.

Shortly thereafter, having munched a couple of cows, Tich disappeared into the heavy timber. And whenever I read Press reports of mysterious sightings of a tiger-like marauder in the Australian scrub, I know that the brute's alive and well.

111

Everytime I come to town
The boys keep kicking my dog around
Even if he is a hound
They've got to stop kicking my dog around.

Champ Clark
(His 1912 Presidential campaign song)

My wife likes animals and the kids are always begging for pets. So I recently bought them a couple of budgies and had them luxuriously accommodated in a huge cane cage. Put together by slave labour in Taiwan, it's a towering structure of pagodas and attics and cost about the same as a modest weatherboard. To show their gratitude, the budgies promptly attacked this Taj Mahal, this Shinto Temple, this ornithological penthouse, devouring the elegant bars as if they were spaghetti. Now the wind blows eerily through the abandoned aviary, mute testament to my accursed and leprous nature. As Shakespeare put it in Coriolanus, nature teaches beasts to know their friends.

I'm His Highness' dog at Kew:
Pray tell me Sir, whose dog are
you?

Alexander Pope, 1730

Apart from lacking a green thumb, I'm certainly no goldfinger, as my most recent catastrophe in the pet department proves. All but deafened by the family's ululations, I agreed to purchase substitutes for the absconding budgies. On balance the least vicious and troublesome creatures seemed to be goldfish. So I visited the neighbourhood aquarium, a place surrounded by lascerating Dayglo signs and pressed my nose to the tanks. There were fish like fireworks, like toffee, like licorice allsorts. There were fish in football jumpers, in filmy lingerie. There were damp squibs and wet dreams.

I first sought reassurance that fish didn't bite the feeding hand, didn't scratch the furniture, didn't do poo-poos on the

112

carpet and wouldn't gnaw through the glass and escape. But it was only when he promised me that I wouldn't wake up at night to find their fangs buried in my throat that I invested in the cheapest goldfish in stock. Two dozen at 65c each. Actually, I suspect they were only eight carat goldfish as they were more the colour of quartz with the odd metallic glint. These were placed in large plastic bags, a straining bladder that wobbled oddly on the car seat beside me. I also bought in weed, pond snails, fish food and a number of recommended water additives.

A few minutes later the fish were safely ensconced in a fountain that, although previously fishless, already abounded with mosquito larvae and suchlike. Whereupon they proceeded to swim around in a satisfactory manner. Yet over the next two days each and every one of them expired. They floated on the surface of the water looking like baleful eyeballs. I tried everything. The laying on of hands, mouth-to-gill resuscitation, rubbing them with Ungvita. All to no avail.

> Ye monsters of the bubbling deep
> Your maker's praises spout
> Up from the sand ye coddlings creep
> And wag your tails about . . .
>
> *Cotton Mather hymn, 1700*

Enraged I returned to that lurid aquarium demanding satisfaction. But the guarantee turned out to be extremely limited: twice around the pond or two hours, whichever came first. I screamed at the unrepentant salesman, that I might as well have bought a few tins of sardines and tossed them into the water. They'd have been just as lively. Finally I stormed out, threatening to report him to Ralph Nader.

I write this column in a sad and desolate home. No birds sing. No pussies mew. No puppies gambol. All I can hear is the sound of children sobbing. I don't know what to try next. It's a toss up between some hardy bacteria or one of those battery-powered monkeys that play the drums.

113

Baldness seems next to Godliness

SPOONER.

Monday's the worst day, when the lads on the assembly lines are feeling resentful about coming back to work. Then your General Motors, Fords and British Leylands produce the so-called lemons, cars that will be plagued with malfunctions. Mind you, the hapless owner has some protection these days, what with warranties and consumer protection laws.

But we can't get much satisfaction out of God, the biggest multi-national of them all, when it comes to legitimate consumer complaints. By rushing the Creation (if only He'd taken a few extra days) it was inevitable He'd make mistakes. Some of the products, like dinosaurs and dodos, were so ill-considered or poorly produced that they've been forced off the market. And the future's not looking too bright for the ubiquitous human, given certain dangerous traits and a quite unsatisfactory service record.

By His own admission, God was guilty of planning obsolescence. Humans were to last threescore years and ten, no more, no less. We've got that in writing, in the Bible's black and white. Threescore years and ten, then off to the scrap yard. Other animals, like turtles and elephants, can do much better than that. And much of the time we don't make even that distance. Millions of us snuff it long before we achieve the guaranteed mileage, owing to defective parts like the heart or the appendix. And does God stock spares? Not on your nelly. We've got to make them ourselves. From plastic and aluminium.

Imagine the uproar if Detroit manufactured cars that fell victim to viruses, little beasties of the corporation's own invention. Imagine if all the Toranas in town suddenly came down with inflamed phoopher valves because of microbes released into the air by a division of GMH. Yet this is exactly what happens with we humans that flood from the Almighty's assembly lines. Quite apart from the high percentage of people with gammy legs and other visible defects, we're subject to catching diseases that He has devised. And it's no good pointing to the threescore years and ten

115

guarantee, because God's got all the small print in the Old Testament. Escape clauses.

The consumer protection people can't touch Him and there's yet to be a successful prosecution under the Trade Practices Act. For my own part, I'd like to sue the Managing Director of Heavenly Enterprises Inc. for such malfunctions as rheumatic twinges, dandruff, headaches, gout and doubts. But what's the use? Arthur Koestler argues that human beings are particularly shoddy pieces of work. On the one hand, our brains are too large, so that we can invent the most extraordinary things like rockets and nuclear weapons. On the other, that part of our brain that gives us morality and judgment is quite inadequate, so that our technological skill becomes a two-edged sword. Koestler sees us as being brilliant morons, doomed to destroy ourselves and our planet. And it's not really our fault. It's God's fault, for jerry-building the entire species.

Let's examine just one aspect of the Almighty's sloppiness. Our naked pelts. All the other creatures were given some sort of weather-proofing, like the rhino's leather, the reptile's scales, the wart hog's bristles, the minx's coat or the orphington's feathers. But we humans were abandoned to the elements in this soft, silly epidermis which is subject to puncturing by prickles, to heat rashes, sunburn, goose-pimples and mosquito bites. This forced us to invent clothing and, worse, to steal the hides and furs from other critters. Admittedly there were other considerations in clothing. Because of God's carelessness as a draftsman, he placed the male genitalia in an extremely exposed position. Not only is it subject to frostbite, but it gets in the way during the gardening. Think of the injuries you can do to yourself, for example, while clipping the hedge. And take the female bosom which, without clothing, poses similar problems in the laundry. Necessity being the mother of invention, the brassière was patented within months of the wringer.

Needless to say our plucked appearance gave us a com-

116

plex. We were ashamed that we alone of God's creatures (with the solitary exception of the earthworm), were lacking leather, quills, bristles, scales or fur. So our shame wasn't a sexual thing at all, at least not at the outset. However, with the passing of time and the invention of religion, things became complicated by guilt, another of the Almighty's lunatic concepts. For just as rust attacks the body of the family sedan, guilt corrodes the human mind.

Now human beings are the only species on this planet who consider the sight of their undraped form scandalous. Nudity is a matter of complete indifference to the gnu, the yak, the tit and the emperor gum moth caterpillar. And if people wish to be nude, they're forced to go deep into the woods and play volley ball or to mount productions of *Oh! Calcutta.*

As an only child, I was profoundly ignorant of the female form. My cousin Terry had bumped me up to a window so that I could peek at one of his sisters in the bath, but her anatomical details were obscured by a rubber duck. And it was no good buying nudist club magaiznes or Man Juniors as the said details were painted out. To millions like me, as to Dylan Thomas, women were a blur below the waist. So it came as a shock to learn about pubic hair, to realise that the Almighty had, after all, allowed grown-ups the odd tuft. And this shock was shared by magistrates the world over who declared photographs obscene simply on the basis of follicles being visible in the immediate vicinity of the pudenda. Inevitably, one got the impression that it wasn't the genitals that were innately wicked, but the hair. Consequently it wasn't cleanliness but baldness of the type observed on Greek and Roman statues, that seemed next to Godliness.

This was an attitude shared even by Hugh Hefner who, until recently, air brushed his Playgirls within an inch of their lives, so that their skins took on the unnatural, unblemished look of a window dummy. (And what a thrill it was

117

to glimpse *those*, when a cheeky window dresser left one naked to the public gaze.)

During the dark ages, only a few pioneers carried the banner of sexual frankness. There were the flashers in the Botanical Gardens and the odd bather who'd brave the insects and the constabulary on secluded beaches. Now, approximately 6000 million years after the aforementioned creation, Hugh Hefner permits coiffed pubes to be featured in his centrefolds and *Oh! Calcutta* has been running in the West End almost as long as *The Mousetrap*. Yet nudity still remains an issue for the primiscuous (a word I've just coined to supersede wowser) who tut-tut about nude beaches and who keep alive the sorts of guilts that have given Kenneth Tynan and Eric Dare their tax problems.

Which brings me, at long last, to the point or points of this all. Having profited from the transvestite boom with *Betty Blokkbuster* and *Flowers,* Eric Dare is now mounting, if you'll forgive the expression, a show called *Let My People Come* (wink wink, nudge nudge). The advertisements feature the sort of elegant typography one usually associates with the ballet or opera but it's my unpleasant duty to tell you that the show is so *awful* that it will put back the cause of volley ball by *decades*. God knows *Oh! Calcutta* was bad enough. Despite the fact that the authors included Samuel Becket, Jules Pfeiffer and John Lennon, the script fell well below the standard that Graham Wigley, Johnny Mason and myself set behind the shelter shed at Eltham High School. Yet the production justified itself because of an exuberance that clearly provided group therapy for its repressed British audience, turning their chill matrimonial mattresses back into joyous trampolines.

Then came a rip-off called *The Dirtiest Show in Town,* which pretended to concern itself with pollution. Once again the cast members were very much in view but the singing was strident and the scripts were even worse. So much so that Barry Humphries and I, who'd attended the show out

118

of a sense of journalistic and theatrical duty, left within ten minutes of the opening. Yet the dirtiest show in town was *Macbeth, Aida* and *Les Sylphides* compared to *Let My People Come* which I saw a few years back in New York, where it was the biggest off-Broadway success. This cynical piece of strip-miming was packing in the middle-class from fifty miles around, shoving them twice-nightly into a fugfilled barn where they sat cheek by jowl on agonising wooden pews. Then, into the spotlight, leapt a dozen or so winter-white Thespians who proceeded to display their bruises, their goose-pimples and their appendix scars along with their genitalia and their minuscule talents.

I seem to remember a succession of bump-and-grind songs with leaden lyrics and a feeling of being had. And it wasn't the nudity that offended, although that was fairly gruesome, but the naked greed of the entrepreneurs. You had a feeling that if violence had been 'in' that year, they'd have sold seats at the abattoirs. I agree with Henry Miller's distinction between the obscene and the pornographic. As practised by Chaucer and Shakespeare, obscenity is a full-blooded and joyous thing, a celebration of sexuality, not an exploitation. But pornography is a mean-spirited business that uses everybody, its performers and its patrons alike. Pornography, as much as censorship, involves the hatred of sex. And *Let My People Come,* for all its arty ads, comes into that latter category. It has all the charm and eroticism of world championship wrestling or a car accident.

Portrait of an artist scaling the heights

Over the centuries, many of history's most ambitious and talented painters have attached themselves to royal or Papal courts where they've turned out umpteen portraits of their powerful patrons. Look at Goya and Velasquez whose genius transformed the Prado into a family album for the Bourbons. Look at Holbein who, having painted Henry VIII, was kept flat to the easel recording his succession of wives. And look at our own beloved Clifton Pugh who, having exhausted our *Who's Who*, now hotly pursues a variety of world leaders. He's already done Golda Meir, is scheduled to paint Prince Philip and has high hopes for Chou en Lai. He's come a long way, our Cliff, since his portraits of crows and wombats.

120

There are those cynics who see Cliff's career as resembling that of a big-game hunter. As the late Wocka Grummet grumbled: 'Instead of stuffing lions and moose for his study, he paints dukes, archbishops and Prime Ministers.' But is this entirely fair? Aren't there a number of unlikely explanations?

For example: whenever he was painting a saint, El Greco would borrow a ratbag from the Toledo lunatic asylum to use as a model. Very pragmatic that. Or is it eclectic? Either way, El Greco had the good sense to realise that saints and lunatics are very closely related, and that lunatics make wonderfully intense subjects. Well, in my experience, a high percentage of politicans and public figures are also mad as cut snakes (paranoia and delusions of grandeur being among the more common symptoms) and are, therefore, equally attractive to the artist's eye.

And there's another possibility. It's not necessarily that Pugh finds the faces of the ordinary uninspiring. He may be concentrating on the mighty out of concern and kindness for his less-established colleagues. For it leaves them free to practise on the working class. Because, with nonentities who's to know if the likenesses are rotten? Then, as they grow in both artistic and social schools, such artists can graduate to the social pages, to the captains and the kings. So it's not fair to brand Clifton as a social climber. He's more of a mountain climber who's daubed his quota of human molehills and is now ready to scale the peaks of celebrity. I mean, you don't expect an Edmund Hillary to go around climbing piles of gravel and sticking flags on humus heaps.

Another thing in Cliff's defence. He comes from a long line of portrait painters who specialised in the mighty. There was Lorenzo del Pugh who painted the Medicis, Anthony van Pugh who painted Charles I of England and Fritz Von Pugh who specialised in kaisers. And we mustn't forget the portraits of Flemish aristocracy by Wilhelm Poo the Younger. For all his obsession with the powerful, it's interesting that Clifton isn't one of your swinging painters. He has a distinct Left-wing bias. It's true that he's painted Archbishop Mannix and the odd Governor-General. But his real preference is for the prominent Labor politican. Take his portrait of Gough for the cover of *Time,* his daub of Don Dunstan for the lobby of the Adelaide Art Gallery. And then there were his paintings of Tom Uren and other prominent front benchers. He's become the Frans Hals of the ACTU, the Rembrandt of the Trades Hall.

But I'm fascinated to know what happens when the subject of one of Clifton's political portraits comes a gutser in his career. Is the portrait of Cairns turned to the wall? Or does Clifton re-use the canvas for a portrait of his successor, just as Madam Tussaud's melts down the heads of world leaders when they no longer figure, so that the wax can be recycled?

So great has been his success, that a Pugh portrait is now considered the greatest honour available to anyone in public life, preferable to having one's head on a coin or postage stamp. 'Any dill can feel the Queen's Wilkinson on his shoulder,' said an emotional Whitlam at the unveiling of his portrait in King's Hall, 'but only the chosen few have been touched by Clifton's brush.'

However Pugh's very success has caused severe personal and political problems, particularly for those he's rejected as subjects. Take the recent suicide of Amy Vanderbilt. It's believed that she threw herself from her Park Avenue apartment when she learnt that Pugh had given her the thumbs down. Meanwhile Henry Kissinger tells me that Pugh is partly to blame for the continuing crisis in the Middle East. Apparently the Arabs are furious that Pugh painted Golda Meir while refusing to do Faisal. 'I'm trying to persuade Pugh to have an even-brush policy in the Middle East,' says Kissinger, 'otherwise another war is inevitable.' But at the time of writing Pugh refused to consider the proposal, even if the Arabs do threaten to cut off his supplies of oil paint.

For Clifton has fatter fish to fry. He is preparing to tackle his masterwork, the first offical portrait of the Almighty since Michelangelo's Sistine ceiling. 'But then,' Pugh explains, 'I'm the first artist of Mike's magnitude since the Renaissance.' Apparently it's all being arranged through Harry M Miller. Clifton will incorporate his great portrait in a new ceiling for Jim Mollison's Canberra gallery, a fresco blending biblical and political scenes. The first segment of the epic work would depict the Almighty reaching down to kindle life in the reclining figure of Gough-Adam. In the next scene Margaret-Eve has been led up the garden path by the serpent and hides her nakedness in a clump of tea-tree. 'I'm unsure about the model for the serpent,' says Pugh. 'But it's a toss-up between Phillip Lynch and Bill Hartley.'

Later Gough reappears as the saviour, surrounded by disciples drawn from his fourth Cabinet. 'Tom Uren will be St Peter,' says Pugh, 'he's got a good, honest, fisherman's face.' As for Matthew, Mark, Luke and John, Pugh proposes using Kep Enderby, Jim McClelland, Lionel Bowen and Moss Cass ('Moss Cass looks very Old Testament,' observes Pugh). Meanwhile Clyde Cameron is anxious to play Judas Iscariot and Don Dunstan has volunteered to be Doubting Thomas. I asked whether the Almighty would be visiting Pugh's studio to pose for this masterwork, this apotheosis. 'No,' said Pugh, 'I'll be working from visions.'

In conclusion, I took the opportunity to ask Pugh how he goes about painting one of his famous sitters. Take, for example, Golda Meir. 'Well,' said a reflective Pugh, puffing on his Petersens, 'I started by giving her a rub-over with a wire brush. Then I filled the cracks with spackle and used a bit of primer . . . '

Somewhere special

As you'll have learned from the excited news reports, I'm off on another expedition, perhaps the most dangerous and challenging of my long and heroic career. But before I discuss the mystery and the magnitude of this ultimate venture, this voyage into the void, this odyssey into inner space, I find my mind wandering back . . . to the time I was awarded the Noble Prize for sociobiology. This is one of the many honours heaped upon my person by grateful society, the others including a Remembrance Day poppy and the *Herald* learn-to-swim certificate. Even now I seem to hear the address given in Stockholm by a member of the Swedish Academy.

Over the centuries man has asked himself many profound questions. Who are we? Where do we come from? Where are we going? And perhaps our greatest achievements in the arts and sciences are a result of such cosmic curiosity. Now a new name must be added to the pantheon of Einstein, Curie, Darwin and Freud. For a man has asked himself one of these great eternal questions and then gone on to provide the answer. The man? Adams of Australia. The question? Where do flies go in the wintertime?

For centuries, nay aeons, philosophers had pondered on that one. During the Middle Ages, even the challenge of alchemy took second place to curiosity about the wintery whereabouts of the blowie. Yet no man, be he scientist or necromancer, had been able to solve this ancient puzzle. Then, in recent years, came a flurry of investigations funded by the Ford and Rockefeller foundations, by the Pentagon and Kremlin. You may recall Professor Harry Messel's plan to feed flies on small isotopes and track their movements by satellite. However, all of the experiments either failed or proved inconclusive; that is, until I came up with the idea of donning a blowie's disguise.

So it came to pass that I purchased an old and rather mouldy fur coat from the Brotherhood of St Laurence, plus a leather pilot's helmet, complete with goggles, from a disposals store. And when I tied two old badminton racquets to my back, the effect was so convincing that I was adopted by the unsuspecting insects and taken back to their secret winter hideaway. Which was, as you'll recall from the resultant controversy, a penthouse in the Mortein factory. Here the blowies wintered in the lap of luxury. They had saunas, a gymnasium, dustbins overflowing with stale crayfish and Mortein executives ready to respond to their merest whim. Moreover, fornication was encouraged so that the fly population would be maximised for the next summer, thus ensuring the Samuel Taylor company's profitability.

But enough of the past. Samuel Taylor have been punished for their wickedness and I have been amply rewarded for my efforts. Now I seek to serve my society in another way – by solving a mystery of even greater profundity. For as you know, I intend finding that special, hidden place where we put things so we won't forget them. How many times have you hunted for your spare set of car keys, flailing frantically around the house, tearing through cupboards, upending drawers and leaving a wake like Cyclone Tracy. 'Damn it all!' you rage, 'I distinctly remember putting them somewhere special so I couldn't lose them.' And when you upend a small vase in the hope of conjuring the key, you get a handful of slimy water. It was the same in the TV licence era. While a cynical inspector lounged in the doorway, you'd thrash around looking in, under and behind. 'I know it's here,' you'd say sheepishly before repeating the stock phrase. 'I put it somewhere special so I wouldn't lose it.'

Prescriptions, important phone numbers, crucial addresses. We invariably put them in this special place so that we won't, *cannot* mislay them. So that we'll be able to put our hands on them *instantly*. And what happens? They're never seen again. It's as if they were sucked into the fourth dimension by a demonic vacuum cleaner. Not only do you lose the all-important thing, but the special place itself disappears. It fades into nothingness, like the Cheshire cat's smile.

It vanishes, dematerialises, implodes. I believe that it has to do with antimatter and quasars and the black holes that scientists have discovered in the universe. I believe that the things we entrust to these special places are somehow whisked to some supernatural Sargasso where they float for ever. Or else they rematerialise in a sort of transcendental op-shop, a purgatory for possessions.

And I'm determined to reach this eerie clime, to discover the whereabout of Auntie Ive's spare spectacles, of my Mum's fluffy slippers, or the refills for my fountain pen. And while I'm there I fully expect to discover forgotten plays by Shakespeare. ('I know I put them fomewhere, Anne, fomewhere fpecial fo I could be fure of finding them again.') And the missing bit of Schubert's symphony. Not to mention the mislaid crew of the Marie Celeste and the girls from *Picnic at Hanging Rock* whom Joan Lindsay so carelessly lost between two drafts of her manuscript. Plus the bit of paper on which I wrote my next dental appointment, plus last year's tax return plus a thing of dental floss plus Lasseter's Lost Reef ('I put it somewhere special . . . ' was the final tragic entry in the dying man's diary) not to mention my library cards.

Come to think of it, the place I'm seeking will have millions of library cards, not to mention odd items like sets of teeth or artificial legs, just as things like that invariably turn up amongst the umbrellas at the Railways lost property auction. ('I distinctly remember putting it somewhere special,' said Douglas Bader as he hopped around his bedroom.)

Even as you read this item, I'll be making a journey into an unknown landscape from whence no visitor or library card returns. In this way I hope to make a future that will be safe for man and his spare set of car keys, not to mention his dry cleaning dockets. I propose climbing into my blowfly costume of fur coat, helmet, goggles and badminton racquets (not that it's appropriate but it's warm) and sitting in my doctor's waiting room where I've so frequently been mislaid and forgotten. Then it will only be a matter of time.

Musings on mortality

a calculator
looks at
life's span

It is the Sabbath morn in Melbourne, that city of Sundays. And while a recording of church bells bellows from yonder C of E steeple, bullying the faithful to their worship, I sit here contemplating mortality. Mine and yours. While the torn cloth over the radiogram's speaker quivers to the sonorous strains and emphatic oomphas of the Death March, I pursue my hobby – tearing hands off old watches. Prior to gelding a grandfather clock by pulling off its pendulum. A melancholic at the best of times, my slough of despond has been brought about by one of those electronic calculators. Already old-fangled in this faddish world, they're a sort of adult counterpart to the yo-yo or frisbee. It's a little pocket-sized effort with illuminated numbers that flicker and prance like a malfunctioning neon sign or, more poetically, like a chorus-line of fire-flies. Having exhausted its interest as a toy, I made the mistake of using it for a series of devastating calculations. The first confirmed the parlous state of my finances whilst the second revealed grim aspects of my life expectancy.

With the exception of biblical fundamentalists who don't believe in that sort of thing, mankind has been evolving for millions of years. Now this process has come to a grinding halt as we leave evolution to our machines. They're evolving instead of us. Take mathematics. While logarithms, equations and such like have always seemed as unfathomable as the cantos of Ezra Pound, I could, with time and enough sheets of paper, perform simple arithmetic. This was entirely thanks to years spent parrotting the two to twelve time tables: 'Three sevens are twenty-wun, four sevens are twenny-ate,' and that sort of thing. But since I got my calculator, this painfully acquired knowledge has faded from the brain, as have my Latin conjugations and at least seven of the Ten Commandments. Verily I say unto you that little by little our gadgets are turning us into morons. And sedentary morons at that.

Anyway, back to the grim tidings revealed by this bastard child of the computer. It all began when I was feeling my usual bitterness about the brevity of our allotted span, in that seventy years is a swizz. We never have the chance to really live. Just when we're starting to get the hang of life, it's all over bar the burying. We're nothing more than transit passengers on a quick trip to the grave. Mind you, some of our fellow travellers are even worse off. Take the little mayfly that lives just a few short hours. Consider the fruit-fly. Probably because it's so cruelly hounded by authorities, its life expectancy is 0.2 years. The Rocky Mountain wood

129

tick does a little better, cashing its wood chips at the age of three. And you won't be surprised to learn that the medical leech (not to be confused with its human counterpart) notches up the longest run of all insects with twenty-four years. The macaw does pretty well compared to human beings, living sixty-four years in captivity. This is rather better than the elephant, which only manages fifty-seven.

And in an interesting comment on Aesop's fable, the race amongst animals goes to the slowest, with the giant turtle nosing past the durable box turtle to reach the finishing line after 177 years. However, given the danger of ending up as a pair of spectacle frames, I'm more envious of a piece of tufa moss, which lives as long as 2800 years, or a Sierra redwood, that can top four thousand.

But as we're reminded by that old adage about rolling stones, moss doesn't get around much. And despite the urging of that popular ballad, few people talk to trees. So it's back to humankind and those stories of epic longevity. But I'm afraid that Methuselah's age was a clerical error (you can't believe anything you read these days) while those stories of Turkistanians or Hindu holy men or Negro slaves living 150 years and more must be heavily discounted.

As it happens, there are only eight documented instances of people living over 108 years and significantly, seven of those were women. However, as far as I'm concerned, even 500 years would be completely inadequate, particularly when you consider the time we waste on things like sleep, feeding the budgie, or taking out the dustbins. So contemplate, if you dare, the following calculations. I cannot guarantee their accuracy as the batteries are going flat.

Our seventy-year allocation amounts to 25,550 days, a figure allowing for the wind and ignoring leap years. By the most optimistic estimates, I've lived 12,505 of those already. But a more careful audit, confirmed by the loading of my insurance policy, reminds me that I can probably knock ten years or 3650 days off that lot, given problems of stress,

130

chloresterol and portliness. So I'm down to 21,900 days for openers. This brings me to sleep, or to the attempt to sleep. Being an insomniac, I rarely get the recommended eight hours, but one still allocates about that time to its pursuit. In any event, most humans spent a full 8516 twenty-four-hour days in a comatose state, which is over twenty-three years! So having given us consciousness with His left hand, he takes it away with His right. Next comes the time one spends in the loo and the bathroom. Add together the periods devoted to cleaning your teeth and worrying about your dandruff — not to mention those moments of blind terror when you find yourself staring at a little cardboard tube bereft of Sorbent — you've spent at least 25,550 hours in those tiled precincts.

I wholeheartedly agree with Bernard Shaw when he said that school interrupted one's education. For my part, school was a purgatory of boredom. Well, assuming that you start school at the age of five and leave twelve years later, you have spent 999.99 days getting ready for, going to, at, coming home from, and doing homework as a result of, that sorry institution. Admittedly there are some joys in education, particularly the things learned unofficially behind the shelter sheds. But by and large they are 999.99 days right down the drain. Whereupon you're faced with a career which usually means hopping on to a treadmill unconvincingly disguised as a bandwagon. Once the novelty of earning the pay envelope wears off, in about a week, you realise you're trapped in an endless and meaningless cycle. And even if you start work at eighteen and retire at sixty, you have spent forty-two years with your shoulder to the grindstone and your nose to the wheel. This means you'll spend 8360 days at work, a figure that allows for holidays but not for overtime.

And that's only the beginning. There's the time you spend getting to the office or wherever. The time (a) levitating in panic as a result of the alarm and (b) pretending you didn't hear it, (c) waiting for the bathroom, (d) lumbering out for

131

the paper, (e) eating your rice bubbles whilst their snap, crackle and pop echoes through your aching brain like mortar fire and (f) trying to find the strength to stir your tea. Then there's the minutes of accelerating desperation as you search for matching socks and car keys and the hours spent in a freeway jam where derisive signs taunt the stationary traffic by advertising speed limits of 100 kmh. In just forty years, allowing for holidays, that tots up to 3193.75 days and we mustn't forget the equally gruelling homeward journey and the numb, limp hour you devote to your partial recovery. So add another 3129.16 days to your running total. Now let us assume that you're sick just one week a year during your schooldays and working life. Not counting the pain or senility or old age, that's 7 days x 55 years equals 385.

What else? Well, television occupies Australians an average of twenty hours a week, with many people notching up more than forty. Given the quality of programmes, this must be considered more a labour than a recreation. Particularly as you're required to memorise the advertisements so as to keep the wheels of commerce turning. A lifetime of that occupies no less than 3120 days.

You will note that I've allocated no time to reading books or walking the dog or making love. There's no allowance for happy years of retirement or for taking *Women's Weekly* World Discovery Tours. On the other hand, I haven't deducted any days for lawn mowing or odd jobs like fixing the cistern. And I should point out that calculations based on a woman's work consume even more discretionary time. Nonetheless, all the foregoing adds up to a (very approximate) total of 27,628.9 days spent doing things that are, to put it mildly, less than joyous. And if I subtract those 27,628.9 days off the 21,900 days I had to start with, two things are agonisingly apparent. Firstly, life isn't worth living. And secondly, I ran out of time 5728.9 days ago. Which means I died in 1961. Thus are we all laid low by a death of a thousand cuts. By all those nicks of time.

Beating the bumps

When it comes to the scientific analysis of the human noggin, I'll take Franz Josef Gall over Sigmund Freud any time. Both practised medicine in the fecund city of Vienna, home of the waltz and the Ferris wheel, where the citizens are full of chocolate cake and the sewers ring to zithers and both were determined to be the Costeau of the cranium, to explore the human intellect, such as it is.

133

Their methods, however, were very different. Where Sigmund tried to sneak into the subconscious via the interpretation of dreams, Franz Josef was content to survey the scalp, taking measurements with tiny tripods and plumb bobs. For he was convinced, as I am, that the shape of the scone and the size and location of its lumps, revealed one's disposition, character, talents, religious attitudes and propensity to crime.

You've heard how Freud was mocked by the medical establishment. That was nothing to the hostility that awaited the infant science of phrenology. First of all members of the establishment took to wearing their hats everywhere, even to bed, for fear of having their propensities disclosed. Then lectures by Gall and his disciple Johann Kaspat Spurzheim were banned throughout the city. You've probably seen a 19th century phrenologist's chart or bust. If you haven't, imagine Yul Brynner's head all covered in dotted lines and notations like: *Ideality, sublimity* and *amativeness.* The region concerned with *destructiveness* is located just above the left ear while *spirituality* and *hope* are side by side along one's receding hairline.

It's hard to see why Phreudianism beat phrenology, given that the former technique takes decades, at $50 an hour, to determine anything. Even something obvious like the fact that you lust after your grandmother. Whereas Franz and Johann could feel your scalp and give you a complete run down in three minues flat. Or have I unwittingly revealed the reason in this paragraph? Could it be that phrenology got the chop because it was cheap, and that Phreudianism flourished because it proved to be the best way of picking a patient's pockets in medical history? I make no allegations.

Anyway, if Franz Josef and Johann Kaspat were alive today, which they're not, having handed in their plumb bobs in 1828 and 1832 respectively they'd find my head particularly fascinating. Because funny little lumps run in the fam-

134

ily. My grandmother had them and her grandmother before her. And so have I. The odd little lump clearly indicative of my commendable ideality, sublimity and extraordinary amativeness.

Apart from coming into occasional conflict with the comb, these little polyps of propensity – or cysts as they're known in Pears Cyclopaedia, the hypochondriac's bible – cause no trouble. But when one's follicles are falling in these autumnal years, when the scalp is opting for nudity, one cannot help thinking about having them removed. Otherwise you'd be wandering around flashing your propensities at every Tom, Fritz and Johann. I mean, what if phrenology made a comeback along with herbalism; your head would be an open book. (This seems a good time to slip in one of those pieces of useless information. The Minister for Health in Sir Henry Bolte's first Cabinet was a trained phrenologist. I refer to the late E K Whately, known to his parliamentary colleagues as 'Bumps'.)

So I visited my local medico who is also somewhat of a friend. Insofar as one can be friendly with a bloke who's forever handing out grim pronouncements on your blood pressure, loathsome prescriptions and prison-camp diet charts. Imagine my surprise when I discovered that, since my last visit to his surgery, both he and it had undergone a mysterious transformation. Just as the signs attacking Medibank had been replaced by framed examples of Chinese calligraphy, Rodney had swapped his formal suit for a vivid caftan and his jar of leeches for a quiverful of needles. As Rodney joyously explained, he had discovered acupuncture.

No longer did he bother to stimulate the phagocytes ... now he preferred to porcupine the patient. Radiant with excitement, Rodney told me that Western medicine was in serious error, that its so-called cures were worse than the disease, and that only acupuncture allowed one to be freed from illness and suffering without being poisoned by chemicals.

135

Rodney told me of operations he'd observed in China, where patients had sung hymns of praise to Chairman Mao during brain surgery and of others who'd danced around the theatre after having both legs amputated. He'd witnessed with his very own eyes Lazarus-and-Lourdes-like miracles where the lame not only walked but joined athletic clubs, where people who'd suffered from migraines for fifty years made a beeline for the commune's discotheque. Inspired by his advocacy, by his missionary zeal, I agreed to having my phrenological features removed under acupuncture anaesthesia. After all, I'd be awake throughout the proceedings, feeling no pain, and would leap from the operating table like Nijinski as soon as the harvest was complete.

Come the great day, I was feeling a little less confident. A lot less confident. To be perfectly candid, I was panic-stricken. And the setting for the operation was scarcely re-assuring. Instead of being admitted to one of those stainless-steel hospitals like in Ben Casey and that Reg Grundy serial, I was ushered into a decrepit old mansion that had been adapted for medical purposes. Thus I found myself laid out under a plaster ceiling rose in exactly the position that had once been occupied by the dining table. True, the nurses had their white drag on, and their face masks, but it didn't feel right. As you know, I'm a stickler for tradition. I believe, for example, that you should be able to tell a pawnbroker's from a boutique: that there should be three brass balls and a windowful of mournful dusty merchandise. Similarly I'd refuse to be buried from an undertaker's that looked like a Colonel Sanders outlet. Yet here I was about to be carved up in a room where, for decades, father had carved the roast. By now my terror had become stark. First needles, now this?

Curling myself inside the sheet, in something between a ball and the foetal position, I called for my Mummy and refused to come out. When I felt the matron's powerful paws upon me, I screamed 'rape' and said I was overdrawn at

Medibank. Sadly these ruses failed and I was soon strapped on my back while Rodney twirled his needles above me like the picador at a Mexican bullfight. Not that his costume suggested the latter as he was enrobed in a full-length dressing gown featuring an embroidered dragon.

As I remember, his first needle acupunctured my foot, either between the toes or around the ankle. The second went in near the knee whilst the third passed into the webbing between the thumb and first finger. And all the time Rodney kept saying that I'd soon feel numbing sensations, that within seconds my scalp would be utterly insensitive to pain. Well, while my foot, knee and thumb began to tingle and throb, as well they might, my head was unaffected. If anything, it became hypersensitive to everything, like an aching tooth.

By now I knew the whole thing was a terrible mistake. I tried to explain to Rodney that I wasn't a suitable subject for acupuncture, that I lacked the serenity of the Oriental or the suggestibility of his other Occidental patients. That just as the great Franquin had failed to hyponotise me in 1951, his needles would fail to penetrate the rhinoceros hide of my scepticism. But Rodney was untroubled. He recounted his long march to medical wisdom and told of the hosts of people he'd successfully treated. He talked of those who'd thrown off arthritis and rheumatism and of others he'd cured of dermatitis, obesity or thrip. I was not to fear as the needles never failed. Indeed, my scone was already as unfeeling as one of those porcelain kojaks employed as phrenological globes. As Rodney twisted his needles so as to hasten the deadening, all sorts of thoughts rushed through my noduled nut. I had a vision of St Sebastian in those Renaissance paintings, simply aquiver with arrows. I recalled the Indian fakirs who lay on beds of nails and remembered the bee-stings from childhood and the way Grandma (the other Grandma, not the one in the fifth paragraph) plied the Reckitt's Blue.

137

Whereupon Rodney hoed into the first cyst with his scalpel. 'There, you're not feeling a thing,' he said. Or rather, shouted over my heart-rending scream. *'I am feeling a thing! I'm feeling your rotten machette!'* 'No you're not.' Rodney shouted calmly, *'The head is completely anaesthetised. If I wished I could saw off your scalp and complete a leucotomy!'*

'Like bloody hell!' I bellowed, thrashing beneath my bonds, *'I'm in agony!'* *'No you're not, you're only pretending!'*

What with my shrieks and his unswerving confidence, we had what could be described as an impasse. East is east and west is west and the twain was derailed on my head. I had only one consolation: that I hadn't accepted his request to volunteer for Australia's first acupunctured vasectomy. Finally Rodney yielded to my entreaties and gave me the one needle for which I yearned, in which I had faith. A hypodermic full of decadent western chemicals that soon had most of me pleasantly numbed. But it was a disgruntled doctor that completed his task. The operation was a success, but the patient was a total failure.

Now my scalp is a phrenological desert. My innermost secrets are safe from the straying fingers of the followers of Gall. But Rodney, undismayed, goes from strength to strength in curing the halt and the lame. And while I find such healing inexplicable, I wouldn't be at all surprised to learn that Rodney has succeeded in raising the dead. If he shoved one of his rotten needles into a corpse it would emit what could only be described as an unholy yell.

The search for Utopia

The Militant trade union leader of the 1890s or the 1930s
or even the 1950s would look at the salaries and conditions
of today's worker with astonishment and disbelief. Has the
Socialist Utopia been achieved? Have all the lads won Tatt's?
Yet despite the great achievements of unionism – the destruction of Blake's dark, satanic mills and the vast increase
in the workers' standard of living – protests and disputes
not only continue but seem to escalate. While the masses
of India and Asia endure their poverty in relative silence,
our unionists angrily agitate for more money, better housing
and domestic gadgetry. For colour tellies and wall-mounted
spin dryers and Toyotas and Ansett holidays at Surfers.

Granted not all unionists are 'little capitalists', a term used
this week by a contemptuous Trades Hall veteran. Some are
committed to worker participation in management if not
outright worker control, while many follow the Swedish
example in seeking alternatives to the tyranny of the assembly line. But more often than not, the motives for mili-
tancy seems petty-bourgeois, recalling the criticism of Welsh
miners by D H Lawrence. Looking back at his life in the
shadow of a colliery, Lawrence deplored the fact that miners
seemed as committed to the capitalist ethos as their employers, that at heart they shared the same dreams and aspir-
ations.

Meanwhile, with one eye on the East, the children of our society protest too. In contrast, theirs is a puritanical stance demanding less, not more. We must, they say, consume less energy and less of our finite resources while living a more simple and austere existence. The only thing in common with these differing logs of claims? The passion with which they're presented to society.

'The more you give the bastards, the more they want' is a familiar complaint of the employer. Yet God knows he's insatiable on a grander and greedier scale, as he orders a dozen oysters Madeleine and an even larger Mercedes, or goes Hilton-hopping around the globe, wielding his Diners' Club card. There's something obscene about a man on $30,000 deploring the 'unreasonable' demands of a miner or a bloke who spends his working life in the thunder of a foundry.

For all that, I believe that the incidence of strikes demands closer scrutiny, that its significance is misunderstood, that the RPM of the rat race is accelerating dangerously, that while people talk of an economic breakdown, a nervous breakdown is as likely and as imminent. Furthermore I believe that it will afflict all modern societies irrespective of their economic system. Even when participatory democracy involves the worker in decision-making, even when automation has made work less tedious and repetitive, workers' protests won't die away. (Look at the social tensions in Sweden which can claim a high level of social justice and enlightenment.) Ultimately it isn't working conditions that enrage us but the human condition itself.

To get to my hypothesis requires a brief detour via Philip Toynbee. Wanting to write a book on human suffering, he ran an advertisement in the London *Times* (thus making a first and tell-tale value judgment) asking people to write to him if they felt themselves to be underdogs. A few days later he was flooded with letters, with agonising accounts of pain and torment. They came from survivors of Auschwitz, from

140

people with terminal cancer, from a woman whose face was hideously scarred, from dwarfs and hunch-backs, from migraine sufferers, from men who'd considered themselves wrongly imprisoned, from covert homosexuals, from guilt-wracked priests, from mothers who'd lost their sons in this or that war.

Toynbee decided to publish a selection of these documents, but found it difficult to choose between them. For it seemed to him that the depths of suffering of his correspondents was not directly related to the magnitude of their problems when judged by normal, objective means. In other words, a girl whose face was disfigured by a birthmark could feel more torment than a quadraplegic. Similarly, whereas many cancer victims cling bravely, tenaciously to life, a physically healthy homosexual might be moved to kill himself. To make matters more complex, two people can respond quite differently to the same nightmares, as emerged in the response from the survivors of death camps. On the evidence of their writing, Toynbee observed that one victim could sail through such an experience, using his innate insensitivity to protect himself, while another suffered, really suffered, the agonies of the damned.

Finally Toynbee decided to make his selection according to the quality of the prose, arguing that the most articulate pieces were also the most deeply felt. It seemed to him that those who wrote in clichés had not been profoundly affected by their experience, where those who'd struggled to express their condition had, of necessity, explored themselves more deeply.

This view finds an echo in Lampedusa's extraordinary novel *The Leopard,* concerning an aristocratic Italian family whose existence is threatened by approaching revolution. The Leopard is the head of the family, a proud and powerful man who numbers among his considerable retinue a personal priest. At one point in the novel, the priest visits his peasant family in Calabria who are suffering as a result of a bad season. Needless to say, at such a time they're waxing both envious and resentful of the aristocracy. Whereupon the priest makes the following, ironic observation. 'For we simple people a bad crop is a catastrophe. But consider the Leopard. For him, a badly ironed collar is a catastrophe.'

Now, Lampedusa and Toynbee are unashamed élitists, and bound up in their writings are some dangerous assumptions. For if it is true that the educated and articulate are more sensitive to everything, including pain, then it follows that the illiterate peasant is anaesthetised by his ignorance. Taken to its logical conclusion, this line of argument would suggest that those countless millions who starve and suffer on this planet are well equipped to do so. And let's face it, that assumption is implicit in most Western attitudes, enabling us to turn deaf ears and blind eyes to the plight of the poor while remaining almost guiltless in our self-indulgence. But look at the young child in pain or misery. He may not be able to describe his pain by written or spoken word, but there can be no doubt of its intensity. Indeed, Toynbee's theory can be up-ended. Perhaps inexpressible suffering is harder to bear and the ability to communicate one's pain eases the burden.

None the less, Toynbee's book – and that anecdote of Lampedusa's – do sound the following warning: as society gives people more affluence and education, it increases their expectations immeasurably and dangerously. Whereas the Asian peasant has perhaps half our life expectancy, and a hundredth part of our income, he's at some sort of peace with himself in an ordered social fabric where the warp and weft are tradition and religion. In contrast, we ride the back of the technological tiger, a man-eating brute who's long since devoured most traditional beliefs. Like so many New Guinean cargo cultists we are taught to believe that material progress would make our lives both meaningful and beautiful. And for the few, short decades it almost worked.

But now? Isn't it possible that some of the stridency of

protest in Western society is more inspired by grief than by greed? That all this anger and disappointment is aimed at the employer and the social system because they provide a ready target? That our real complaint is with the meaninglessness of human life and with the terrors inherent in mortality?

D H Lawrence argued that the real enemy of the workers was not capitalism but industrialism itself. Increasingly, this is also the message of our children. They insist that industrialism replaces qualities with quantities and that its new products have turned out to be poor substitutes for old values. Certainly the Utopia that Western society believed was in its grasps has turned out to be something of a fizzer, like Evel Kneivel's symbolic Snake River rocket. All we've got in return for our heightened awareness and our increased expectations has been a deeper and more profound depression. And while I use that word in its emotional rather than its economic sense, there's probably some significance in its double meaning.

Despite the missionary fervour of sundry gurus, more and more of us live in a meaningless world, without the consolation of faith, according to a materialist or humanist or existentialist philosophy. At the same time we live in a world increasingly preoccupied with death. And surely at no time since the plague-ridden Middle Ages has that spectre been so omnipresent. Subsequently I believe that many people who go on strike are making demands that no employer can meet. For what they're demanding is a sense of cosmic direction, for some meaning to their existence. Read between the lines of the placards in the hands of the pickets and you'll see the same words: 'Is this all there is?' Man has built his civilisation simply because he is never satisfied. Thus the cave and mud hut evolved into the cathedral and the skyscraper. Thus your common-and-garden millionaire feels poor in the presence of a Rockefeller or Getty. And spends his life accumulating money he can never hope to spend.

Other men try to run faster or climb higher or love more women or amass the world's largest collection of Toby jugs. Yet in the end there's always exhaustion, boredom, a sense of anti-climax. Hence that bleak, black question: 'Is this all there is?'

It's a luxurious question that only the developed nations can afford to ask. You don't hear it in Chad where the per capita income is $60 a year or from Ceylon where it's $150 or from Nigeria where it's $70 or from Paraguay where it's $200. But you do hear it from the workers on assembly lines and the bosses wives on tranquillisers. Increasingly it is the querulous and frightened cry of advanced, industrial society, where mass production has failed to deliver the goods.

The man in the long white coat...

Carruthers had been showing signs of strain for months. One moment he'd be irritable; the next he'd laugh uncontrollably. But his fellow directors were sympathetic. After all, it wasn't easy to be the secretary of a major stockbroking firm at a time like this. The news of BHP's collapse had been a shock to all of them. However, when Carruthers began quacking at board meetings and signing 'Donald Duck' on company cheques they knew he needed more than sympathy. And so Carruthers was taken to a discreet psychiatric clinic based on the avant-garde theories of Dr Emil Fossbinder.

On his arrival Carruthers was met by an extremely attractive young matron and taken to a viewing room above the group therapy area. 'Don't worry,' Carruthers was told, 'they can't see you. The other side of the glass is mirrored.' And he was invited to study his fellow-patients for a few moments while the principles of the treatment were explained.

Carruthers was astonished by what he saw. There below him were hundreds of the most famous people in history. He saw Beethoven, Marie Antoinette, two Hitlers and Hopalong Cassidy mingling with each other – and with a grotesque twenty-stone woman squeezed into a tu-tu and an equally obese old man crawling around in a nappy.

'It's incredible,' murmured Carruthers. 'Like a carnival, a circus. As if Madame Tussaud's had come to life.' 'It's all those things,' said a powerful voice behind him. Turning, Carruthers saw a man in a white coat standing in the doorway. 'But most of all it's an enormous fancy dress party where you can choose to be anything or anyone you like.'

'But I don't under . . . ' said Carruthers. ' . . . stand? It's all based on Dr Fossbinder's theories,' said the nurse. 'You see, he had a large and very successful practice among the European jet set.'

'And I can assure you that their numbers include a great many very disturbed personalities,' said the doctor. 'Fossbinder was fascinated by the fact that the wealthy adored throwing fancy-dress parties at their chateaux and palazzos – where they could hide their everyday personalities behind fanciful costumes or magnify them in some appropriate uniforms. He also observed that such parties seemed to have exceptional therapeutic value – and that the choice of costume was very revealing to a trained psychiatrist.'

Carruthers watched while Florence Nightingale joked with Sherlock Holmes and Dr Watson. He saw Einstein writing equations on the blackboard and a reasonable facsimile of Captain Hook molesting Goldilocks.

'How come,' asked Carruthers, 'that you have two Jesus Christs?' 'It's a particularly popular costume,' explained the doctor. 'However, they've come to an equitable arrangement. You see, the one on the right's the Second Coming.'

'In ordinary life one is forced into conventional clothing, required to suffer the petty tyranny of suits and ties. Even women find that fashion imposes all sorts of restrictions. So one really can't express oneself. But at my fancy-dress ball a housewife can be Cinderella and Jekyll may be Hyde.' Whereupon the nurse threw open the doors of a very large cupboard and said: 'It's time for you to choose.' Carruthers was confronted by the most fantastic variety of clothing.

'We get all the old costumes from J C Williamson's,' said the matron as the doctor fondled her bum. 'And from the television channels as well.' 'Dr Fossbinder also spent a fortune when MGM auctioned their wardrobe,' added the doctor. 'However, if you like something special – something we don't have in stock – we'll be glad to run it up for you and charge your company's account.' But Carruthers gave a little quack of joy and reached out to touch a garment of feathers with long pipe-stem legs and floppy, webbed feet. 'Donald Duck?' asked the doctor with a little smile. 'You *are* going to be a hard nut to crack.'

A few minutes later Carruthers was waddling behind the matron to meet his new friends. While clearly suspicious of her, Sarah Bernhardt, Ned Kelly and Plato shook his wing enthusiastically. But Carruthers couldn't help feeling uneasy about the anxiety he saw in their faces. Was there perhaps some other aspect of the treatment, something painful? But Carruthers put it out of his mind as he preened his feathers and practised his Donald Duck voice in a friendly conversation with the front end of a pantomime horse.

'I don't suppose you'd be interested in moving in with me – safety in numbers and all that?' the front inquired. 'I had hind-quarters, but when he started bucking the system the doctor had him removed to another ward.' Straightening his sailor's jacket and adjusting his cap, Carruthers declined.

As the days passed Carruthers learned that the patients

loathed the doctor and greatly feared his daily rounds. As the hour approached all gaiety faded and people fell quiet and huddled against the walls. Carruthers also noticed that while the doctor was indifferent to the less aggressive patient, to those in fantasy or fairy-tale costume like his own he was very unpleasant – even cruel to Napoleon Bonaparte and to the two Hitlers. On one occasion Carruthers saw the doctor bullying Captain Bligh until he'd reduced him to tears.

'He's a cruel and savage monster,' said an octogenarian Superman. 'He insults us, starves us, beats us,' whimpered a one-legged Fred Astaire. 'What's more he charges us the most fantastic fees,' said Dickens' Scrooge. 'I think he's *awful*," said the 5 ft. 2 in. Goliath. 'Then why not do something about it?' asked the duck. 'Why not leave?' 'We can't leave,' they chorused. 'We've all been committed here by our families or our companies. We can't leave until he says we're cured.'

For all his desire to escape the burden of executive decision-making in favour of the innocence of duckdom Carruthers felt his hackles rising. 'We can't take this sort of thing lying down,' he said. 'We must stand up for our rights. We should get together and form a deputation.' At this suggestion the normally supercilious Queen Victoria dithered while Tarzan muttered something about a torn ligament. Whereupon Carruthers tried to shame Lenin and Stalin into taking political action, tried to inspire Thomas Jefferson with talk of Liberty and Freedom. But none of them would follow him.

Then, suddenly Carruthers found himself being frog-marched to the doctor's office. 'I hear you're trying to organise some sort of mutiny,' the doctor shouted at him, plucking a handful of his feathers. 'Never mind who told me, I have my sources.' (Not that Carruthers doubted the source for a moment. He'd been warned to keep an eye on Judas Iscariot.) 'Well it's shock treatment for you, Carruthers,' snarled the doctor as soon as they were alone. 'I'm going to skewer you on a rotisserie and cook you. Then you'll be moved into the ward downstairs with that horse's arse and the other hopeless cases.'

'What gives you the right,' spluttered Carruthers through his yellow bill, 'to treat us like this?' 'This white coat gives me the right – that's what,' roared the doctor. 'Which is exactly why I picked it when I arrived – instead of some dopey cowboy suit.'

The corpse's revenge

When Hercule Poirot walked onto the stage, he did so without fanfare or introduction. Indeed, the famous Belgian detective had been standing in the spotlight for some seconds before the audience became aware of him. Whereupon an utter silence passed across the crowd. And as though it had been a cloud, it was accompanied by a chill. With his fussy, anachronistic clothing and his waxed moutstachios Poirot looked, as always, absurd. Yet if the presence was incongruous, it was also commanding. As was the gesture he made to the wings. Instantly two policemen appeared wheeling a trolley, covered with a white sheet. Beneath it you could see the outline of a body, a large body. Poirot gestured again and more policemen appeared, their arms full of weapons. There were guns, knives, swords, nooses, bottles of poison, blackjacks, bombs.

'All of these weapons were found by the body,' said Poirot. 'Any one of them might have been responsible for his death. Just as any one of you in the audience might be his murderer. It is not my custom to deliver the *dénouement* of a Poirot case in such a vast chamber. I prefer the claustrophobia of a saloon car on the Orient Express. Or the elegant living-room of a country house. But this case is, of course, rather different. We needed to hire this Opera House to hold you all, the primary suspects. For it quickly became apparent to me that the victim had many many enemies.

151

Some of you were proud and defiant in your hatred and spoke openly of your joy in his demise. Others of you were hypocritical, feigning loyalty when you'd yearned and plotted for his destruction.'

I looked around at the familiar, even famous faces in the hall. Some frowning, most expressionless. And they watched Poirot with unblinking concentration, the rise in tension was palpable.

'You, Malcolm Fraser, were high on my list of suspects,' said the detective, suddenly pointing at a tall man in the front row. 'Not only did you hate his beliefs but you are a poor match for his intelligence and eloquence. In debate he could and did humiliate you. Many people here have already decided that you are the guilty one.' Poirot snapped his fingers and a spotlight shafted down from somewhere high above. 'Whereas others, Sir John, accuse you,' said Poirot as the light sought out those ruddy, heavy jowls. 'For did not the victim curse you from the steps of Parliament House and shun you at official functions? Did not he ridicule you at a hundred public meetings? And was not the Black Rod, the symbol of the Queen's authority, the authority vested in you, found beside the body? It is hard to imagine a more formidable bludgeon – or for that matter, a man who'd be more willing to wield it. Yes, Sir John, like the Prime Minister you conjured into existence on November 11, you must expect to be suspected.

'And you, Mr Hawke, for all your protestations of solidarity, is it not true that you wanted the deceased out of the way? So that you might make your run for the leadership? Are there not signs that your power base is eroding? Have you not been planning for many years to assume a safe seat? Despite the hostility of Caucus to the notion (they believed that a new member should serve an apprenticeship on the back bench) haven't you believed that they'd turn to you in desperation? May you not be, therefore, the principal beneficiary of this man's downfall? And was not this spanner, branded ACTU, found beside the body? And is this not the same spanner you threw into the party's works when you so readily confirmed the allegations of Iraki money? It is true that your motives are not entirely self-seeking for you have a true affection for the Israelis, the bitter enemy of your party's proposed benefactors. But it is your vaulting ambition that placed you high upon my list of suspects.'

Now Poirot clasped a manicured hand to his brow. 'But how many of you there are! Men like you, Monsieur Connor. And your comrades, Messrs Crean, Cairns and Cameron. Dishonored, disgraced, discarded, dismissed.'

During this outburst the spotlight veered around the hall, seeking out each man in turn. 'Oh yes, you have many reasons to hate the deceased. For while protesting his own integrity, he cast so many aspersions on your own. You were mighty and have fallen. Any one of you might have been his assassin. And you, Monsieur Hartley. You began your career as a Young Liberal and with the passage of time, have become more and more the radical. You who support Arafat and his revolutionaries. Would you not prefer to see your party led by the Left rather than the bourgeois figure who now lies beneath this sheet? You, who have no patience with moderation, with fence-sitting? I'm sure that at least one of the weapons lying here could be shown to bear your fingerprints.

'Now to you, Monsieur Murdoch, who publishes newspapers across the globe. It would seem that you too hated this man. You like to think that you played a major role in his gaining power – although I would suspect that you were merely swept up by the same inexorable forces. Be it as it may, you have turned against him. Why? Did he refuse to honour you in the way you deemed appropriate? Did he refuse to pass legislation that you deemed appropriate? Certainly you made no secret of your growing enmity. But perhaps you went too far in your campaign. Many of your colleagues saw your performances as obsessive. Now, as a

153

result of your enthusiasm, you face a succession of libel actions. *Mais oui,* monsieur. Your invitation to this gathering was well deserved.

'Madamoiselle? Madame? Ah, excuse me, *Mzz* Read. I'm unfamiliar with the nomenclature preferred by your women's movement. You too have some reason to hate the deceased. He lifted you from obscurity but then broke your crusader's sword. And cast you from him. Like Comrade Hartley, you're engaged in revolutionary struggle, and the man who promised you his support abandoned you. Were you the guilty party, one might almost talk of a *crime passionnel.* But, as a man who believes in the old notion of chivalry, however repugnant that might be to you, I must say that I have always believed in your innocence.

'This brings me to you, Monsieur Holding. After all, you are the State leader of your Labor Party. You are engaged in a State election and in a fight for your own political survival. I can imagine your anger at recent events where, once again, your Federal leader has sabotaged your chances. I think we could understand it if, in your fury, you had struck out at this man. Then there are you, Messrs McMahon and Snedden. Did not the deceased make you both look faintly ridiculous, thus sealing your respective fates? And you, the gentleman sitting in the far corner, beyond the reach of our spotlight? Are you perhaps the culprit? After all, you are from the CIA, an organisation dedicated to the downfall of Leftist parties and their leaders.

'But I could go on and on. I could refer to Monsieur Barnard whose reward for loyalty was public humiliation – or to Monsieur Bowen who shares a fierce ambition for the leadership. Or to you, the mild-mannered Moss Cass and Gordon Bryant who hated the man beneath this shroud for his arrogance and dictatorial behaviour. For conduct unbecoming to the leader of a democratic organisation. Did you not wield knives when Caesar fell? Might not *your* blow have been the mortal one?

154

'I'm sorry that I have not referred to all of you by name. But you will appreciate that there are so many people who wished this man dead, who'd be proud to take the responsibility. In a strange, perverse way, your hostilities are a measure of his magnitude. In my short time in this country, I have learned of the traditional hostility to those regarded as 'tall poppies'.

'Well, who is the guilty one? Which one of you is the killer?' At this point Poirot began to walk around the stage, looking into the audience, while the spotlight flailed across the faces and the audience lifted their arms to protect themselves from its brutal flare. 'It is my conclusion,' he said finally, 'that none of you did it. That this man, this extraordinary, paradoxical man, this Whitlam, died by his own hand. And by his own mouth and by his own ego. All of you tried in your own ways, but you failed. You lacked the strength, Monsieur Fraser, Monsieur Hawke. As for you, Monsieur Murdoch, you are not as powerful as you imagine. This man Whitlam, he destroyed himself.'

This was followed by a different sort of silence. While Poirot's judgment sank in. Then a resplendent, bewigged and rather silly figure stood and introduced himself as Bill Snedden, Speaker of the House.

'Sir, I just want to say that you've done this audience a mis-service. For whatever we might have thought of the deceased, we are men of probity and distinction. And I can assure you that all of us deeply regret Mr Whitlam's untimely demise. His loss diminishes us all and Australia is the poorer for his passing.'

And just as the audience was hear-hearing that noble sentiment, the figure on the trolley moved, sat up and began to struggle with its sheet. Whereupon a voice cried from the audience: 'Oh, my God, the bugger's *still* not dead'. And, led by the Speaker hurdling the seats, his robes flying, the entire audience rushed the stage, shrieking like girls at a Stones' concert.

SPOONER.

Terror comes cheap at the supermarket

Last week my wife got stuck in the half-lotus at her yoga class, so I had to go to the supermarket. However, I'm responding well to treatment and should be out of intensive care by the weekend.

You're far safer walking through Harlem at night than you are going to Dickins in daylight. As for the carnage at Supa Valu, Safeway and suchlike, it exceeds both the death toll on the Hume Highway and Australia's losses at Gallipoli. Subsequently RSL membership should be expanded to include returned shoppers, while room is found at the Shrine for the tomb of the Unknown Housewife.

While the bloodshed begins in the car park (where women battle for possies with the determination of Israeli tank commanders in the Sinai), the real savagery begins once we pass through the turnstiles. Here mild-mannered members of mothers' clubs and Christian congregations become harpies and anthropophagi who lash at each other with string bags or claw at eyes with lacquered talons. Invariably their rage is rekindled by the trolleys. If not in short supply they're locked together as if copulating, either circumstance provoking vicious tugs-of-war and fish-wife obscenities.

But I'm getting ahead of myself as I'm still trying to nego-

157

tiate the aforementioned turnstile. So much is the supermarket a woman's domain that these chromium carousels are designed to geld the interloping male. One must either pass through *en point,* as they say in ballet circles, or attempt to vault. Affecting nonchalance, I decide upon the latter.

Picking myself up from the floor, I find no shortage of trolleys. Indeed, I'm confronted by a sort of metal millipede stretching for about thirty feet. However, after much tugging and grunting the trolleys are still hopelessly enmeshed: whereupon I espy a solitary trolley standing by the plastic buckets. I might have known. It turns out to have a club wheel that not only wearies the wrists but produces a banshee wail and a determined veer to the left. Subsequently you find yourself ricocheting off the displays or other people's trolleys, usually in a shower of sparks. Worse still, you're incapable of turning right for the budgie seed or muesli listed on the back of your torn envelope. Instead, you're doomed to orbit the store in an anti-clockwise direction like a malfunctioning Sputnik. Mind you, most of the trolleys are as battered as Boadicea's chariots after her routing of Rome's 9th Legion. Apart from missing wheels and dents, you see pieces of bloodstained clothing wedged between the wires, souvenirs of fatal head-ons by the freezer cabinets.

As it happens, I narrowly escape being mortally sandwiched between two harridans closing in on the last packet of Special-K, whipped to a frenzy by the blood-thirsty urchins sitting twixt their handlebars. So as to vent their spleen on the consumers, the owners of supermarkets spent years studying the Hampton Court maze and the Cretan labyrinth before opening their doors. Consequently it's a virtual impossiblity to find anything. Hence the pitiful wrecks who wander around in ever-decreasing circles on bleeding feet, muttering 'sultanas' and 'soap pads' in hopeless voices through cracked lips. (They've formed a sort of skid-row down by the Pine-O-Kleen and White King stands, building

158

humpies from cardboard boxes and living on Good-Oh and Vita-Brits stolen from the shelves.)

Danger is everywhere. Even if you survive the muggings in the dark aisles and the pile-ups at intersections, there's the constant threat of an avalanche. You reach out for a tin of Heinz's baked beans, only to be inundated by their remaining fifty-six varieties. This is because all displays have been deliberately booby-trapped. (Note that the TV cameras that sweep the stores are *not* to discourage shoplifting. Instead, they relay one's slapstick progress and discomforts to a roomful of chortling supermarket employees.)

Worse still, the gauntlet of the check-out awaits you. According to Freud, one of the most common reoccurring nightmares involves fleeing from a monster of some sort, only to realise that you're running on the spot. And you feel much the same sensation when trying to lift things out of your trolley for the cashier. This is because she adds things up so quickly that she's always hot on your heels. Or to be more accurate, hot on your fumbling fingers. And heaven help anyone who falls wheezing at the wayside. Terrible stories are told of those who fail this penultimate test. In supermarket circles it's regarded as a more serious offence than shoplifting. Not only are your goods confiscated but you're dragged screaming to the manager's office and worked over with a salami.

Once you've passed the register, you're then left with a pyramid of packages and no assistance in sight. A cashier may call 'help at four' through the microphone, but no help will come. This leaves you causing a traffic jam with your yoghurt and teddy-bear biscuits getting mixed up with the next customer's teabags and margarine. So you set off in search of a box.

Now, you've been through a lot in the past thirty minutes. There were the cruelties of the car park and the traumatic tug-of-war for the trolley, not to mention the bloody collisions and the blinding agony of those cascading cans.

But none of this will have prepared you for the inhuman savagery of the battle of the box. Supermarkets always ensure that there are nowhere near enough cartons to go around, so that you're forced to hurl yourself into the ravening hordes. And if the scene in the car park was reminiscent of *The Cars That Ate Paris,* this reminds one of the closing seconds of Tennessee Williams' *Suddenly Last Summer* when poor Montgomery Clift was eaten alive by starving Mexicans. And if you do emerge victorious, you know that the box is cunningly designed to fail you twenty feet before your boot, where it will open like a bomb-bay causing the tomato sauce to haemorrhage on the rice and spilt milk.

We're proud of our social progress, that horses no longer are sent down mines, just as children are no longer sent up chimneys. Yet we tolerate a situation where our wives are forced into these hells-on-Earth, these establishments worthy of Eichmann. So don't ask for whom the till tolls. Supermarkets stand condemned as symbols of man's inhumanity to woman.

Peace to all men on dustbin night

As you'll probably have noticed, we live in a world of conflict and unrest, a world fragmented by race, colour, creed and ideology. And at times it seems we're destined to slip into some terrible abyss. But I thought I'd bring you all a message of hope. For just the other night I learned that the human race is one and indivisible after all. I was suddenly made aware of the unbreakable links and bonds between us all.

This extraordinary insight — this spiritual awakening — occured last Thursday as I was dragging our dustbin down to the front gate. It was a dark, windy night and to bolster my spirits I was humming *Onward Christian Soldiers* when, all at once, I realised that countless thousands, indeed millions of my fellow citizens were engaged in the same domestic ritual. All around me unknown neighbours were lumping their dustbins to their front gates, unconsciously sharing in the common task and destiny.

And suddenly the lyrics of that stirring hymn took on an urgent relevance:

> Like a mighty army
> Moves the Church of God
> Brothers we are treading
> Where the saints have trod
> We are not divided
> All one body we
> One in faith in hope
> and one in charity.

What a sense of unity and purpose that awareness gave
For perhaps the first time in my life, I knew that no
was an island, that each of us shared the same burden,
encased in PVC or galvo. And consider what a great
is the dustbin night. It's wonderfully egalitarian. No
hat one's station in life, each of us must carry his
his respective front gate.

I'm reminded of the profound lyrics of another

song, of *The Bluebird of Happiness* as performed by John Charles Thomas. 'The beggar man and the mighty king,' Mr Thomas sang, 'are only different in name. For they are treated just the same by fate'. How true. How very true. For the very moment I was wheezing along with my bin, there was every possibility that Mal and Tammy were struggling towards the front gates of the Lodge with theirs. Just as Sir Doug Nicholls was in Adelaide and Mr Bjelke-Petersen was in Brisbane. Just as Sir Henry and Lady Winneke were in Melbourne and Bob Hawke was in Sandringham.

As I straightened my back, I could feel them straightening theirs in turn. And somehow I knew we were all gazing upwards at the same inky heavens, before returning inside to snib our fly-wire doors. And I hope you won't laugh if I say we seemed to be linked together telepathically. It was almost as if the handles of our dustbins had linked together to form a mighty chain. There are some of you who will not accept the beautiful philosophy of *The Bluebird of Happiness*, who will argue that beggar men are forced to eat from the dustbins of the mighty. Moreover, you may argue that not everyone takes their bins out on Thursday night, that some make that pilgrimage on a Monday or Tuesday or Wednesday.

But these are petty criticisms. After all, soldiers have to break step when crossing a bridge, least their pounding boots set up powerful rhythms that might endanger the structure. Clearly if we all took our dustbins out on the same night, it could cause minor earthquakes. Imagine what would happen if 600 million Chinese took their dustbins to their front gates at exactly the same time on Thursday night. Without question Japan would be devastated by tidal waves. None the less, it is safe to assume that a great percentage of the world's population were taking their bins out on that particular evening. Just as they have on Thursday nights since

163

the dawn of time. Consider the Pompeians found buried alive at the doorways of their villas, their terracotta dustbins grasped firmly, eternally, in their hands. Waiting for the dust-chariot that never came.

So it was that I stood there, listening to the darkness. It seemed to me that, from across the ocean, I could hear the Queen and the Duke of Edinburgh panting as they carried their sizeable bin to the front gates of Buckingham Palace, where the guard in his sentry box snapped to attention. And I was conscious of President Carter dragging his bin down the long, concrete path to the gates in Pennsylvania Avenue. Meanwhile, thousands of miles away, Mr Brezhnev was closing the Kremlin's gates, having left his bin against the wall in Red Square.

(Mind you, it's even worse if you're a grazier like Fraser, where your front gate can be a hundred miles from the house. To catch Thursday's collection, you'd have to leave home on Monday morning.)

As a child I found it very difficult to believe that film stars took out their own dustbins or, indeed, that they went to the lavatory. However, on my last trip to California I saw all the dustbins outside their mansions in Beverley Hills. Even more exciting, I actually saw Greta Garbo greeting her garbo. She must have forgotten to put out the bin, as from the bus window we caught a glimpse of her running down the drive in her dark glasses calling out to the garbage men in her thick Scandinavian accent. But it was too late. The truck roared down the Santa Monica Boulevarde and she was left standing there, looking alone and vulnerable. Incidentally, most film stars have bins of characteristic shapes. Thus Liberace's is inspired by a piano stool, Fred Astaire's looks like a top hat and Dean Martin's resembles a champagne bucket.

Which reminds us of the American journalist who earned his living by going through the garbage of celebrities. He wrote a series of columns for *Rolling Stone* in which he revealed what he'd found. From memory, Bob Dylan's bin was full of heroin needles, while Nelson Rockefeller's was jammed-packed with small change.

But I'm drifting away from the real significance of dustbin night. For my Thursday experience stresses how silly it is for nations to fight and argue. Just as there are messages in bottles, there are messages in dustbins and they speak to us of peace and good will. Subsequently I see each and every Thursday night as an opportunity for us all to bury our differences, just as our councils bury our refuse. As we march together towards the front gate we must also march towards a common goal.

For my own part, I resolve to treat each and every dustbin night as a sort of sacrament, as an opportunity to salute my fellow man. In the immortal words of that beloved Australian poet, C J Dennis, I dips me lid.

The boys in blue go pink

This is the time of year when cicadas shed their crisp, brown corsets and abandon themselves to pleasure. It is also the time when constables doff their blue uniforms to feign homosexuality, in the hope of bringing deviates to justice. Overnight the long arm of the law (or 'lily law' as homosexuals affectionately dub its custodians) becomes limp-wristed while its heavy tread feigns the characteristic and coquettish mince. The lads then loll around the lintels of leading loos or disport themselves upon our beaches, poised to pounce upon the flirtatious poof. It's a tactic that has drawn flak from civil rights leaders and from the spokespersons of gay organisations.

They point out that the police are being provocative in at least two senses of the word, as the technique involves enticement as well as entrapment. Thus a respectable married gentleman who has managed to repress his tendencies for years might suddenly yield to the mink and moue of a particularly lissom bobby. (Something similar happened last year to my uncle Aubrey while overseas. He'd taken the trip to celebrate the sudden death of Aunty Maud and while wandering around New York's Central Park taking snaps with his Instamatic had become separated from his group. An unworldly man, Aubrey was unaware that just as most of America's communists are members of the FBI, almost all the women in the park are transvestite policemen intent on luring rapists. So on attempting to take a snap of a particularly comely matron, he found himself charged with molesting an Irish constable from Queens. Fortunately everything worked out all right, as they subsequently married and are now living happily in California.)

I'd like to criticise the vice squad technique of proffering constables as jail bait, but from a rather different point of view. For today I speak in my capacity as honorary treasurer of the Royal Society for the Prevention of Cruelty to Policemen. Isn't it bad enough that we have them stand in the middle of intersections inhaling carbon monoxide without expecting them to drench themselves in oil of patchouli aftershave? Isn't it enough that we expose them to the physical danger of confrontation with bank robbers without exposing them to the moral dangers of encounters with amorous window-dressers? To roster police for such duties seems a quite improper use of the official truncheon.

A letter to the Editor has speculated on the type of toilet training that must be going on in our police stations. Young men of impeccable background and fine sensibilities are exposed, indecently so in my view, to information and diagrams beyond their sexual ken. Little wonder that men often become traumatised and spend the rest of their careers in the force rushing into shops and arresting statues of Michelangelo's David or Beardsley drawings.

There's another aspect of this controversy that hasn't been publicised, an oversight I shall now hasten to correct. To retaliate against policemen disguising themselves as homosexuals, *homosexuals are now disguising themselves as policemen.* Literally hundreds of Victoria's finest are, at the present time, fairies.

I first became suspicious when I noticed that our previously pristine police cars were suddenly emerging from Russell Street in a kaleidoscope of pretty colours. Violet, lavender, mauve. Next I observed young constables on the beat flaunting marcasite handcuffs and listening to Judy Garland records on their two-way radios. But final confirmation came when I heard the siren on a Schiaparelli pink prowl car. Instead of wailing in the approved manner, it was playing *My Heart Belongs to Daddy.* When hardened criminals were dragged into HQ for questioning, one used to hear thumps and muffled cries. Now all that can be heard when you press your ear to a blackened window are wild shrieks of laughter and muffled giggling. Furthermore, large numbers of criminals introduced to homosexuality at Pentridge are now giving themselves up and forming queues for interrogation.

Clearly the public must be warned. If you find your car is being followed by a motorcycle, I urge you to increase speed immediately. Do not, repeat *not* pull over. If a constable tries to sell you tickets to the Policemen's Ball, and you've no wish to see a room full of men dancing with each other, invent a previous engagement. And should a man dressed in police uniform come to your door and ask you to accompany him to the police station, hide under the bed. On second thoughts, hide under something else. And when the opportunity presents itself, make a bee-line for the local public lavatory and appeal to a homosexual for help. Almost certainly, he'll be a policeman.

Upside down life
of an insomniac

Not to be confused with the drumming of cicadas – that sound so evocative of Australia's summers – circadian rhythms are every bit as insistent. For they dictate the metabolism of all species, be they amoebas or prime ministers, oysters or elephants. Because of circadian rhythms, dictated by the Sun, everything on this Earth has periods of activity and inactivity. We wake and we sleep. Or rather, you sleep. For reasons I cannot fathom, my circadian rhythms lack this tidal tidiness. Instead they veer and vacillate like St Vitus dancing to some tipsy tango, robbing me of awareness on the one hand and rest on the other. Thus I drowse through crucial meetings while staring at the ceiling rose all night.

I've tried every known folk remedy, beginning with the counting of sheep. I've taken census of flocks large enough to restock the entire Riverina, flocks that would awe Sir William Gunn or Dalgety and Co. Yet for all the woolliness of their forms and the hypnotic qualities of their numbers, this enumeration of Merinos has proved futile. So I've tried counting other countless things like second-hand Holdens or leaders of the Liberal Party. And while that's been somewhat anaesthetic, while it's given my sleeplessness the extra dimension of acute boredom, it hasn't cured my insomnia.

Apart from reading myself bedtime stories I sing little songs to myself like *Mr Sandman* and *Sleepytime Girl*. I croon lullabies to me, like Brahms' *Cradle song* or *Sleep Now my Little One, Sleep.* Far from rendering me unconscious, such nocturnal recitals wake up my wife. Whereupon things congenial or, if you prefer, conjugal, frequently follow. But not even this brings oblivion. I find myself even more awake and twice as exhausted. This brings me to night-caps. I've tried them all. Hot cocoa and brandy and warm milk. I've gone to bed awash with Bournvita only to toss the night away. I've gone to bed aslosh with Remy Martin, but the only effect has been that I slur the lyrics of my lullabies. Shleep now my liddle one shleep.

Toss the night away? Toss is hardly the word for it. My bed becomes a trampoline. I make it buck and heave just like those scenes in *The Exorcist*. Not content with thumping the pillow, I bully the blankets, strangle the sheets and mangle the mattress. After eight hours I stagger out of the bedroom as if I'd just gone eight rounds. I was tempted by a water-bed but it's out of the question. It would be like a storm scene by Turner. I'm afraid it will be much the same when I'm dead. People on their way to weed Aunty's plot will hear bad-tempered noises rising from the loam. Instead of resting in peace, I'll be down there getting shirty with my shroud. Perhaps that's why so many tombstones are askew; they belong to insomnial corpses.

The longest recorded period for which a person has gone without sleep, while under medical surveillance, is 282 hours 55 minutes. This was a Mrs Bertha Van Der Merwe, a 52-year-old housewife from Cape Town. Then there was the strange case of Mr Eustace Rushworth Burnett, who was born in Leicestershire in 1880. He claimed to have lost all interest in sleep by 1907 and never went to bed until his death bed at the age of eighty-five. But my position is quite different. I *yearn* for sleep. I lust after it. It is my ambition to challenge the world record for snoring, which stands at sixty-nine decibels. (This was recorded at the Ear, Nose and Throat Department of St Mary's Hospital in London in 1959.) Yet I am doomed to spend the nights listlessly turning the pages of magazines or staring glumly into the refrigerator.

For a while I took the kind advice offered by Moss Cass, the only Federal Minister who did house calls. He told me not to worry. Just accept that you're an insomniac and relax. So I'd lie there humming and smiling in the dark and feeling sorry for those wasting precious hours in the arms of Morpheus. (Morpheus is the god of dreams and not to be confused with the author of *Certain Women*.) But all the time there was a little voice inside yelling out 'liar!' So then

I tried the advice of David Martin, the distinguished and somewhat eccentric novelist. He'd been a fellow sufferer until he tried reversing the stress. Whenever he couldn't sleep he'd lie in bed telling his mind that he *wanted* to stay awake. And given the perversity of the subconscious, he'd be out to it in no time. But my subconscious proved only too amenable to this suggestion. The result was instead of being awake but sleepy, I was *awake*. I might as well have been popping amphetamines.

Finally I took the advice of my wife, who goes to yoga classes where she ties herself in reef knots and clove hitches. She said I had to *command* my body to sleep. So I'd lie there commanding. 'Toes, go to sleep!' I'd say, 'feet, go to sleep!' And I'd slowly work my way up past the ankles and the knees towards the bonce. It worked fine, except by the time I got to the navel my toes would wake up again. I was faced with an endless task, like the painting of the Sydney Harbour Bridge.

Things having reached crisis point (I seemed to spend the day ricocheting off office partitions and stifling yawns), I decided to take pills. So I obtained a prescription for a brand so virulent that nine out of ten Hollywood stars use them for their suicide attempts. But where they took Marilyn through those Studio Gates in the Sky, they merely added a surreal dimension to my restlessness. The ceiling rose began to pulse like an anemone. The bed posts went up and down like the brass poles on Luna Park's merry-go-round. Yet the sandman failed to sprinkle the required granules into my stark staring meat pies.

So much for the night. As I've hinted, the walking-hours are a misnomer. It doesn't really matter if you zizz off on the freeway as the bumper-to-bumper traffic propels you in the general direction. Things become really difficult when I arrive at the office as no sooner is the first meeting of the day in progress than I find my vision blurring. Moments later I topple into my coffee and have to be lifted from

172

drenched agenda papers. Mind you, it's even worse on aircraft. Twice or three times a week I stagger aboard a seven or eight o'clock flight to Sydney. No sooner am I confronted with the TAA breakfast of powdered egg and fried bread (fried bread! they must have a shearer's cook left over from the Depression) than I feel an overwhelming desire to lose consciousness. Mind you, the TAA breakfast is notorious for making passengers lose all interest in living. Whereupon I drowse until roused by the Musak that signifies an imminent landing. Of course, there are other reasons for feeling sleepy whilst aloft. It may be an attempt to deal with subconscious terrors. Or it might be that the humidicrib atmosphere of the Boeing, wherein you're as helpless as a premature baby, brings back the drowsiness of one's first weeks. Indeed, the steady roar of the jet engines might evoke prenatal memories. A gynaecologist tells me that the baby is soothed by similar noises as corpuscles course through its mother's placenta.

There's another place where I invariably fall asleep. And that's the theatre. Having spent my early years reviewing plays for the *Bulletin* I find that, to this day, my lids close as the curtain rises. Perhaps I could hire out-of-work thespians to peform *Hedda Gabler* in the bedroom. Perhaps I could call midnight meetings at my beside (well, Lyndon Johnson used to call Cabinet meetings by his bath or while he sat enthroned on the loo) or I could have my wife bring me a TAA breakfast on retiring while playing sound-effect records of DC-9s.

Combined with *The Three Bears*, my yoga exercises, my hot toddies, my drunken lullabies and the chloroform my wife is putting on that wad of cotton-wool, it ought to do the trick.

The unmaking of a teenage Bolshevik

I'd read and re-read all the Biggles and Billabongs and knew the Williams off by heart. So like Oliver Twist walking nervously towards the beadle to ask for more gruel, I looked up at the council librarian and asked for a more interesting book. She knew that I'd exhausted the possibilities of the children's section and decided to turn a blind eye to the regulations. After a few moments' consideration, she gave me a volume from the grown-ups' library. It was *The Grapes of Wrath*, by John Steinbeck.

I read it once, twice, three times, marvelling at the power of the words and thrilling to the anger of Steinbeck's denunciations. After those images of injustice – of food being destroyed while people starved, of farm houses being levelled by the bulldozers, of the murderous brutality of police and vigilantes – Sam Katzman serials and Superman comics seemed very timid stuff. I was at once devastated and exalted by the book for it promised to give purpose to my life. Perhaps I couldn't believe in God, but I could believe in Steinbeck's cause. Instead of wallowing in self-pity, I would join in his crusade against oppression.

Thus, at twelve years of age, I became a convert to radicalism. I was the shelter shed subversive, the playground polemicist, trying to educate the prepubescent masses into political awareness, trying to turn them from an empty life of bread and circuses. Or rather, of Violet Crumbles, hot dogs and football. Needless to say, I was unsuccessful. However, in the course of my crusade I became friendly with a boy called Carl Andrew who'd read *The Grapes of Wrath* at eleven. As rejects from the footy team, we were able to hold long discussions on sports days, and it became clear to us that capitalism was a monstrous, indeed carnivorous, social system that must be destroyed. Then, and only then, could the meek inherit the Earth.

The only trouble was that I didn't know any communists. So I sought them out at the Yarra Bank where, each Sunday, they competed with the Catholic Evidence Guild, various Biblical fundamentalists, the quixotic loners and the loonies, for the attention of the indifferent or the derisive. And there was one communist speaker in particular I admired, a rather striking middle-aged man who, whilst all fire and brimstone on the stump, had a kindly face. After a few Sundays I made my tentative approach. He seemed astonished at my interest. But then, this was at the height of the Menzies, McCarthy and Cold War era when to be identified with the Communist Party was asking for trouble.

As I was subsequently to learn, it was asking for police harassment, for phone tapping, for ASIO to lay dossiers on the desks of prospective employers and for visa applications to be vetoed. Most of all, it was asking for a paranoic sense of being both a martyr to the truth and a victim of persecution by *them*. Not that the position we faced could be described as inexplicable or unreasonable. After all, the organisation was dedicated to overthrowing the social order, so you could hardly expect the establishment's wholehearted co-operation. Or for them to make cash donations to the floating fund. To my astonishment, my Yarra Bank orator declined to grasp me in his arms and call me Comrade. If anything, he was actively discouraging and, worse still, rather amused. Was I sure that I had a political vocation? Mightn't mine be a momentary enthusiasm? It seemed to him that my attitudes to politics were very romantic. And in any case, I was too young. By now I was fifteen years old and full of certainty. So I persisted, until he took my name and address and said that someone would be in touch. Don't call us, we'll call you. And within a few weeks, someone did.

Two men called at my home and, much to my mother's surprise, asked if they might discuss some private matters with her son. Then followed a long interview, almost an interrogation, which I suppose was intended to evaluate my motives, sincerity and sanity. For my part, I found my two communists something of a letdown, for these members of the local branch seemed more concerned in pressuring the council over drainage than they were in storming the barricades. None the less, I must have passed their test because, after little of what the Catholic Church would describe as instruction, and having lied about my age, I was admitted to the Greensborough branch. I was sixteen years old when I joined and was to stay in the party for three turbulent years, resigning to protest at the purging of a number of friends because of their opposition to the invasion of Hungary — and their 'I told you so' reactions to Khrushchev's denunciations of Stalin at the party congress.

Yet that wasn't the only reason. I resigned because of my

discovery that, for all its claims of rationality, the party was a *religion*. And if I couldn't believe in God, it seemed inconsistent to belong to an organisation that, in so many ways, seemed an echo or even a parody of Catholicism. I soon learned that for every hardliner who'd joined the party as a result of hunger-marching in the 1930s — or as a consequence of front-line experience in the factories – and for every scholar who really had read *Marx* – there were a dozen like me who desired to fill the vacuum created by agnosticism through some temporal system of belief, some secular faith.

Subsequently branch meetings weren't the sinister, chthonian gatherings imagined by the establishment, but more like a mother's club or a Sunday school gathering. Complete with tea and home-made scones. There was a quality of innocence, of earnestness, with endless discussions of the need to organise money-raising barbecues or raffles or to increase the weekly sales of the *Guardian* from twenty copies to a thumping twenty-five.

Of course, someone would always deliver a political report on national or world events, but this was invariably composed of approved catch-phrases and clichés, like the sales pitch at a Tupperware party. But revolutionary zeal was conspicuous by its absence among people who could, by and large, be described with that most dreadful of epithets, nice. In any case, apart from their unusual concern for the plight of their fellow man, they were generally conservative in their tastes and their morality. Plaster ducks were not unknown on their walls, nor Mantovani records on their gramophones. And they tended to tut-tut their disapproval of any extramarital goings-on among the membership. As for their ability to undermine capitalism, they'd have been hard-pressed to raffle that legendary chook in a country pub.

When I think back, eighteen years later, I'm amazed how funny it all was. Not so much funny peculiar or funny ha-ha as funny *sad*. I remember groups of the more sophisticated

177

party intellectuals – the ones who were expelled in the late Fifties for various heresies – discussing, *seriously* discussing, whether Australia would be a communist State by 1960 or whether it might take until 1962. Not that they were silly enough to imagine, as did the National Civic Council, that there might be popular uprisings among the workers. Although they were to scorn the domino theory during the Vietnam war, they were in fact domino theorists themselves and believed that Australia would be surrounded by communist societies and that, therefore, we'd have revolutions by osmosis rather than guns.

I remember a meeting at which those of us involved in the arts were read the ideological riot act. It was held at the New Theatre in Flinders Street and various members of the audience were required to stand on stage and deliver reports on the local party's successes in the ballet, in literature, in painting. I can remember looking glumly at a banner stretched across the stage that read: 'Broaden contact with the masses.' *Broaden* it? We didn't have any contact with them to broaden. Our publications and tracts were about as eagerly sought after as copies of the *Watchtower*. Whilst to sell someone a copy of the *Guardian* was about as difficult as serving a subpoena.

The intellectual level of the discussions at the arts conference was typified by a stentorian attack from the lectern on that 'Right-wing fascist surrealist William Dobell', which our artist-laureate Noel Counihan did his best to refute from the floor, explaining that Dobell wasn't exactly a fascist or a surrealist, and that the same man's work was being attacked by the establishment. Not that our apparatchiks took Counihan's defence very seriously. After all, some of his paintings showed distinct revisionist tendencies and were moving into areas beyond the strict bounds of socialist-realism. Meanwhile, one of my expelled comrades, now a very respected educationist, belonged to a branch where the

178

secretary was a local builder while most of the members were his own labourers. And he recalls frequent attacks from the chair on the innate dishonesty of the Australian workers who keep 'pinching their bosses nails'.

All in all, the local comrades were more like Abbie Hoffman's yippies than members of Lenin's cell, in that they had a talent, albeit unconscious, for political absurdity. Take the serious clashes during this period that took place on bridges or in railway culverts where the Left and the Right duelled with paint brushes. 'Out Bob' we'd paint which they'd promptly amend to 'Our Bob'. Whereupon we'd make it 'Sour Bob'. Hardly the sort of thing to shake the nation to its foundations.

As for the success of communists in trade unions, it always seemed to me that this was misinterpreted. To a large extent, workers were pragmatists who'd vote for a communist in their union whereas they'd never vote communist at the State or Federal elections. Even in the wharfies' electorate of Melbourne Ports, a commo was in danger of losing his deposit. I suspect their reasoning went something like this: a commo won't leave the union for his own financial advantage and he won't become a bludger like some of those Labor blokes. Moreover, many commos were imaginative and innovative men, like Seelaf in the Butchers' Union, who established a first-class hospital for the lads. But then, they had more need of medical attention than most, given the problems between cleavers, mincers and fingers.

I doubt that the Communist Party achieved very much in the Fifties and Sixties. At best they were ineffective, at worst counter-productive. Their efforts through front organisations to end the Cold War were, inevitably, symbolic as Australia was about as relevant in the scheme of world affairs as Patagonia or Liechtenstein. Thus when we chanted 'ban the bomb' it was more a prayer than an effective protest. (Compare this to the UK where the marchers were concerned with banning the British bomb – a relevant and even feasible objective.) The peace movement in Australia wouldn't have an urgent role until the anti-conscription and anti-Vietnam struggle when we supported the USA with our ventriloquial foreign policy.

As for being counter-productive, I'd suggest that the CPA greatly assisted the National Civic Council by providing a couple of Reds to put under beds. And this, in turn, gave the DLP its *raison d'être* and helped keep Labour out of office. If the CPA made a positive contribution, it was almost in spite of itself. For it spawned a phenomenon known as the New Left, made up of defectors and of intellectuals excommunicated by the Stalinists. Having wasted years by living in a political fantasy that looked to Moscow for its inspiration – which, for Australian purposes, was about as irrelevant as looking to Mars – they became more perceptive, more sceptical. And members of the New Left were to play a significant role in helping the ALP revamp its policies so they'd seem more acceptable to our middle class. In particular, the New Left tended to identify the new issues that would capture the public interest in the late Sixties and early Seventies – issues like capital punishment, censorship, the arts and that carry-all category known as the 'quality of life'. For the ALP, like the communists, had tended to concentrate on traditional monetary and union issues that simply bored the wider, younger electorate who'd never known financial hardship in their lives. At best, like me, they'd read about it in *The Grapes of Wrath*.

Yet I regard the time I spent as a teenage Bolshevik as invaluable. It replaced the tertiary education I couldn't afford with some extraordinary experiences, while developing my sense of the ridiculous. I emerged from the encounter with a profound suspicion of ideology which, while giving one a direction, also fits you with blinkers. (I forgot to mention that comrades were expected to read the impropaganda of a Howard Fast whilst turning a deaf ear to the writings

180

of, for example, Bertrand Russell.) And see how proudly blinkers are being worn these days, by everyone from Billy Hartley to Malcom Fraser.

If it was necessary to pay royalties on a quotable quote, the executors of Bernard Shaw would have profited considerably from his adage: 'If you're not a communist by the time you're twenty you've got no heart – and if you're a communist after twenty you've got no head'.

I wish I'd said that.

The twin religions

During my teens, I spent a lot of time at the International Book Shop buying the approved novels of Howard Fast (who was later to recant in *The God that Failed*), plus the odd volumes of Marx which, to this day, remain unread. Next to Joyce's *Ulysses* and Chomsky's *Aspects of the Theory of Syntax*, I find *Das Kapital* the least comprehensible of tomes.

There I'd notice racks of cheaply printed tracts, bearing the imprimatur of the Kremlin and depicting the up-turned face of Vladimir Ilyich Lenin. This illustration was done in such a way as to make Lenin look transcendental, not merely a man but a Messiah. And often, at lunch times, I'd sit in St Patrick's Cathedral enjoying the reverberant silence while admiring the soaring elegance of that commendable Gothic pile. And here, built around a massive column, I noticed another rack of tracts that seemed identical. Once again there was an official imprimatur, the typography was identical and the paper was similarly cheap. Except that this time the cover showed the face of Christ in an almost identical pose.

So when I broke with Bolshevism in 1956, at the age of eighteen, largely because I'd discovered the Communist Party to be a religious organisation in secular disguise, demanding one's unquestioning faith and obedience, I arranged an exchange. I swapped Lenin's tracts from the International with those at St Patrick's, so that Left-wing readers were asked: 'Why not be a nun?' while Catholics were warned of the dangers of revisionism. I don't know how many members of the Eureka Youth League finished up as novices nor how many members of Archbishop Mannix's congregation switched allegiance from the Vatican to the Kremlin but it did seem that I was making a legitimate point. At very least, about the nature of propaganda.

At the moment, the world is watching anxiously as the Catholics and the communists battle things out in Italy. Admittedly, Italy has a very sophisticated Communist Party which, like France's, claims to be independent of Moscow. (While the French have abandoned the hammer and sickle, the Italians are showing their subtlety by running Catholic candidates.) But equally, there are forces within the Vatican that are anxious to break down the image of Catholic intractability, by making minor concessions to the spirit of liberalism.

So it still seems to me today, as it did almost twenty years ago, that the two powerful, multi-nationals who compete for the allegiance of millions, are in many ways like two sides of the same coin. Despite the schism between their isms, they've more in common than either would like to admit. For a start, there's a tendency for Catholic countries to produce enormous communist parties, as both Italy and France show. Oddly enough, a significant percentage of the Italian communists still regard themselves as being good Catholics, although their church takes a different view.

In the Fifties, I learnt that communists looked to Moscow for direction just as Catholics look to Rome. In particular, they looked to the Kremlin which, like the Vatican, is a State within a city, and to the word of a leader elected, like the Pope, by a very limited franchise. For Stalin, Khrushchev or Brezhnev was held to speak for communists with the infallibility of *il Papa* speaking to his international flock.

Indeed, it's only a matter of time until the party secretary's election is announced with a puff of red smoke.

Both isms derive from a Judaic tradition and both have their Old and New Testaments. For Moses, read Marx. For Christ, read Lenin. For the apostles and disciples, read the Bolsheviks who supported Lenin, the man who now lies in state in that holy of holies, the red granite tomb by the Kremlin walls. Where he's worshipped by an endless queue of the faithful, who wait in line from summer through the freezing snows of winter. Waiting more patiently than the pilgrims who line up for the catacombs outside Rome or to see the tombs below St Peter's. And above them, on the spire of the Kremlin, like the light over Bethlehem, is a neon star. Both isms have striking symbols. One the cross, the other the hammer and sickle. Lenin, like Christ, achieved his place in history by identifying with the meek and the humble. Their means were, of course, profoundly different with Christ teaching peace while Lenin argued for revolution. But then, one was offering heaven in Heaven while the other thought it possible to achieve heaven on Earth. Communism has borrowed the notion of instruction from the Catholic Church, requiring would-be members to be prepared for admission to the organisation by inquiries into their motives, sincerity and readiness. And communism, like Catholicism, uses the weapon of spiritual exile. For as purges in Prague have dramatised, to be expelled from the Communist Party has repercussions as serious as excommunication from the Church.

Both organisations have a vast professional hierarchy, dedicated to the proposition of the meek inheriting the Earth, to the notion of the equality of man before God or, in the communist case, before society. Yet both have had to face the problem of aristocracy, of some being more equal than others. In Moscow, there's a bureaucratic class who enjoy a wealth of privileges, just as Rome has its cardinals who arrive at the Cavaliere Hilton in their chauffeur-driven

Rolls. In Yugoslavia, Tito's friend Djilas went to jail for writing about the so-called new class, just as Jan Hus was barbecued for accusing Rome of decadence and corruption.

The church has, for centuries, been very concerned with the dangers of heresy. In its short history, the Communist Party in the USSR has been just as anxious to stamp heresy out, except that they call it revisionism. And both the Church and the Communist Party must contend with the trendies – the former with Holland's radical bishops while the latter has the French and Italians rewriting Lenin. Historically both structures have faced even greater challenges. Just as the church had difficulties with Martin Luther and Henry VIII, the Kremlin had had to cope with the insults and criticism of Chairman Mao who thought they'd sold out.

Both Catholic and communism are vast multi-national operations with a tendency to adopt the characteristics of the local society. Thus the Catholicism of a peasant in Calabria differs greatly from the Catholicism of Teddy Kennedy at Hyannisport, just as Catholicism's political stance varies from relative radicalism in southern Africa to ultra conservatism in Spain. And it's the same with the Communist Party which could, until recently, not only count among their members countless Asian labourers but the millionaire Picasso. And there's a great difference between the political styles of, for example, flamboyant Cuban communism and the almost monastic severity to be observed in Albania. Thus terms like Catholic and communist are almost useless as definitions. To have any relevance in a theological or political discussion, both terms need to be qualified. What type of Catholicism? What sort of Communist?

Both isms have, of course, their hymns. For make no mistake, the Internationale is most certainly a hymn. And both have their heavy-handed official art which tells the faithful what to think and feel. Admittedly the Catholic Church has produced some magnificent official art while the communists still slog away with those dreadful social-realist paintings. Not to mention those insufferable revolutionary ballets that the Carters and the Frasers are forced to applaud on visits to Peking. And both surround their holy places with kiosks selling plaster statues of their respective saints, while in Russia the birthday of Lenin serves as a sort of Christmas Day. And there's the way both parties have been known to dismiss saints – as recently happened when the Vatican withdrew their commissions from Saints George and Christopher on the grounds that they had never existed. (They were, in effect, clerical errors.) Which is what Moscow did at the time of Khrushchev, when it decanonised Stalin on the grounds that he too was a non-person.

And in both St Peter's Square and the Red Square, the faithful form huge crowds and look up at a waving figure on a balcony. Both religions like grandiose architecture – Rome building its cathedrals whilst Russia creates its appealing Palaces of Kulture. And as well as their saints and martyrs, both have their Judases, the Russians call theirs Trotsky. Both isms have their moderates, their fanatics and their zealots and both have succeeded in the world because of their sense of purpose, of destiny. For both believe that all other philosophies are in error and must be vigorously opposed. And both have hierarchies that have, from time to time, become tragically remote from their congregations or populations.

Yet for all their disagreements, both the party and the church share a similar attitude to morality. For a moment in time, the Russians might have thrown out bourgeois morality along with capitalism, but when a lady at the party conference suggested that sex was like water 'and when you're thirsty you drink' Lenin retorted with 'yes, but not from a dirty glass'. This prime response precipitated the USSR into a period of sexual repression worthy of the Festival of Light. Meanwhile, both organisations share a great tradition of censorship, publishing their long indexes which oddly enough, were sometimes in agreement as to undesirable films.

And just as the church has had its inquisitions, the communists have had their share of trials requiring public confession and recantation. And for every skeleton in the catacomb, there are skeletons galore in their respective closets. For example, both the church and the party have, in both historical and recent times, been accused of antisemitism. And both dismiss inquistions and other atrocities as being irrelevant, saying 'we cannot be judged by them'. In time, they deplore such unfortunate occurrences while insisting that they were but momentary detours on the long road to truth. And of course, both seem to believe in the perfectability of man, either here or in Heaven, something that sceptics like myself cannot for a moment accept. For even if man did somehow stumble upon an ideal society, I'm sure he'd have mucked it up by tea time.

Of course, each organisation hates the other. Yet both will sit down and work out schemes of arrangement. This can be observed in Poland which remains both Catholic and communist and will be seen, I suspect, in Italy. And each of them, each of the monoliths, is subject to the same tensions and dissensions, to the same sort of attack from within and without forcing them into change where their instinct is for conservatism. And while both parties will certainly object, I believe that the same sort of historical pressures have, from time to time, produced a need for similar styles of leadership. Take the earthy, lovable John XXIII who spoke out for negotiations with the communist world – while his contemporary Nikita Khrushchev, earthier still, argued for peaceful co-existence. Both men followed remote, austere leaderships – just as both have been followed by a conservative backlash.

And most of all, both juggernauts are facts of life and death on our hypertense planet who must find out what else they have in common. That's the least we can ask of our two most influential religions.

For Christ's sake?

In the vampire movies beloved of necrophiliacs and children, Count Dracula is easily put back in his box. What kryptonite does to Superman, what Mortein does to blowies, the crucifix, when waved aloft like a tennis racquet, does to the toothy Transylvanian. With unconcealed, uncongealed horror he backs off hissing like a punctured tube until it's a relatively easy matter to skewer his heart.

Oddly I seem to have the opposite effect on those who wield the crucifix. There are a great many Christians who see me as the Antichrist, and when they're not threatening the Editor with cancelled subscriptions, they're threatening me with brimstone. A few weeks back, Senator Button sent

189

me copies of a letter that he and every other Federal parliamentarian had received, demanding that I be silenced thirdwith while an *Age* secretary was astonished to hear your author being castigated from the pulpit of her local church. But then, any number of public and prayer meetings have been held to protest my sinister influence.

Then there were the epistles gleefully describing the eternal barbecue awaiting me, correspondence I thoroughly enjoy. Which is more than I can say for the letter of forgiveness that arrived, characterised by cloying prose and accompanied by moronic tracts. Unsolicited forgiveness, particularly when you've no intention of seeking it, can be extremely irritating.

The drift of the correspondence from Christians, whether enraged or conciliatory goes something like this:

(a) Christ is the way – the only way – the truth and the light.

(b) All other philosophies and religions are in tragic error and without Christianity there is no hope for the individual or for the world.

These points are expressed with the utmost conviction, in a tone of voice that brooks no argument. Apparently it's also self-evident that only the wilful or the wicked cannot see it. You'll observe that they recall the stance of Malcolm Muggeridge on *Monday Conference*.

It's much the same with the sort of mail I get from communists who are also ready to damn me if I criticise the repression of Jews in the USSR or, for example, the Chinese paranoia over the Antonioni documentary affair. And if you try to explain your lack of enthusiasm for *their* theology by referring to the invasion of Hungary or Prague, the brutalities of Stalin or the vast crimes conducted against humanity in the labour camps, these are airily dismissed. Just as a Christian will brush off references to the Inquisition or the Holy Wars or the pogroms. For such events are but momentary aberrations that in no way diminish the ultimate truth of Christ, Lenin or Mao as the case may be. For your true-believing communist, mock trials and torture and the monstrous tyrannies that characterise Eastern-bloc regimes must be disregarded as the people responsible are not *true* communists. Even if they dominate and direct the activities of the Communist Party, one is to ignore them as unrepresentative.

Equally, the Christian will argue that one should ignore the sort of Christianity that inspires, for example, the castrating, cross-burning racialism of the Ku Klux Klan or which justified the white supremacist convictions of the Boers. Equally, one should ignore the brand of Christianity that gave Franco such unstinting support or the Christianity that, in Addis Ababa, turns a deaf ear to the cries of Ethiopia's starving because they happen to be Moslems. And the same applies to the sort of Christianity that justified the butchering bombs of Belfast, just as we're supposed to forget the ravings of carnivorous generals who, for decades, justified the carnage in Vietnam in Christian terms, who saw that monstrous, genocidal folly as a latter-day crusade.

Consider the following. The Christian judges communism by its works, by its cruelties, and not by its professed ideals. Yet, when it comes to assessing the role of Christianity in the world, we're expected to do the opposite – to ignore the atrocities committed in Christ's name and to look at the religion's ideals. We're expected to believe that, at any minute, *true Christianity* will emerge triumphant, shaking off its horrible history like a butterfly emerging from an ugly chrysalis.

You may remember a TV games show called *Tell The Truth*. In it, a number of anonymous people would claim the same identity. For example, four men would insist that they were Harry Bloggs, taxidermist. Following a cross examination by a panel seeking the truth, the studio lights would be lowered and some mysterious music played. Whereupon the compere would call out: 'Would the real

191

Harry Bloggs please stand up'. And the four contestants would shift in their seats, teasing the viewer until the last second. Then, finally, one man would rise to laughter and applause.

Christianity's a bit like that. A vast game of *Tell The Truth*. George Wallace tells us that he's the real Christian, as does Carter, Herbert W Armstrong and Billy Graham. As does Ian Paisley and the chief of the IRA's bomb squad. As does Ian Smith and the Lebanese lads who've been blazing away at the local Moslems. And if you were to cry out; 'Will the real Christian please stand up,' they'd all stand up, some of them with their hands around each other's throats.

Well, just how *do* you pick a Christian? Identification is made difficult because the teachings of Christ are almost invariably ignored by those who profess to follow him. For example, Christ said: 'Resist not evil . . . turn the other cheek' (not that this was a new idea – the same philosophy had been expounded by Buddha and Lao-Tzu). Yet Christianity and Pacifism have long been strangers. Right from the outset, evil has been identified with great enthusiasm and crushed by growing armies of Christian soldiers.

Then there was the way Christ said: 'Judge not lest ye be judged.' Yet Christian justice has built a forest of gibbets and a multitude of jails and concentration camps. When it comes to passing judgment, moral or otherwise, you can't beat a Christian.

I know that there's always a gap between aspiration and achievement: 'Between the ideal and the reality falls a shadow.' But in the case of Christianity – as in the case of Communism – that shadow seems very dark indeed. Between the time of Constantine to the end of the 17th century Christians have butchered non-Christians with an energy and dedication that makes the Roman persecution of their fledgling religion (slight, intermittent and wholly political) seem like good-natured horse play. When they haven't been

192

destroying Jews or Moslems, they've been burning witches or mincing each other – always in the names of God and Christ.

Christians, like Communists, judge their religion by the standards of fantasy. Judged by the facts, Christianity's contribution to the progress of mankind has been, to say the least, debatable. It promised love and brought us an intensification of hatreds of intolerance. It talked of unity and oneness and gave us the divisiveness of sectarianism. Yes, I know of individual Christians whose contribution to mankind has been of great significance. But equally I know of atheists whose integrity and example has been ennobling. All that that proves is that the world produces a few extraordinary men and women who escape the gravitational pull of crassness and self-interest. Similarly the principles that notionally guide our community (like 'Thou shalt not kill' and 'Do unto others') are not exclusively Christian. They're plain common sense.

Malcolm Muggeridge can write his head off about Sister Theresa's work in Calcutta, but he should remember that it was Christian hostility to the notion of birth control that made contraception a forbidden subject in universities and research laboratories around the globe. In this way Christianity has helped put this planet at risk while intensifying the suffering of millions. Writing about Muggeridge, some time ago, I conceded that there is much in Christ's teaching that is moving, compelling and profound. But not everything Christ said seems eminently sensible. I must complain about the fears and terrors that Christ has put into this world when he talks of 'the damnation of hell'. For Christ says, among other things 'the Son of Man shall send forth his angels and they shall gather out of his kingdom all things that offend, and them which do iniquity, and shall cast them into a furnace of fire. There shall be wailing and gnashing of teeth.' Like Bertrand Russell, I believe that this doctrine of hell fire as a punishment for sin is a doctrine of cruelty, a doctrine that has unleashed untold misery and generations of cruelty by inquisitors and their ilk.

By all means point to Christianity's majestic cathedrals. I too find them awesome and magnificent. At the same time they remind me of the soaring Tambaran houses of the Sepik River, sacred places built by native craftsmen to house their totemic figures. It is not patronising to say that these buildings are, were, among the most astonishing on earth. Yet until very recently, it was the practice of Christian missionaries in New Guinea to burn them to the ground, such was their contempt and hatred for an ancient, fragile culture. Needless to say, at the same time, the missionaries forced Christian clothing upon the villagers' bodies and Christian guilts into their minds.

Of course one must be awed by the Christian contribution to music, to art, to architecture. If only Christianity had returned the compliment to the achievements of other religions. It's not only in the jungles that Christianity's official vandals have destroyed sacred buildings and statuary. Everywhere you travel in the ancient world, you find the monuments and the 'idols' defaced (and often depenis'd) by the triumphant church. And when visiting the Vatican museum or the Prado, to see the dazzling array of chalices and reliquaries containing the teeth or the dandruff of this or that saint, you know that much of this gold was pillaged from the Incas by the all conquering Conquistadors, after the sort of self-righteous carnage that was to characterise Christian imperialism for centuries. These were the same Spaniards who, in Mexico and Peru, baptised the Indian babies immediately prior to murdering them, arguing that this secured the infants' immediate entry into heaven. And don't try and tell me that such monstrous cruelties are behind us. Listen to the patriot's defence of Calley and Co., after the My Lai massacre and you hear echoes of the same obscene logic.

While Malcolm Muggeridge probably rejects Bertrand

194

Russell as a dirty old man, I'd like to quote him at some length:

> You'll find as you look around the world that every single bit of progress and humane feeling, every improvement in the criminal law, every step towards the diminishing of war, every step towards better treatments of the coloured races, or every mitigation of slavery, every moral progress that there has been in the world, has been consistently opposed by the organised churches of the world. I say quite deliberately that Christian religion, as organised in its churches, has been and still is the principal enemy of moral progress in the world.

Of course, my criticisms of Christianity can be applied to some extent to other religions. Such as Buddhism where the simple purity of the founder's philosophy became distorted, decadent in the hands of priesthood. On his death bed the amiable Buddha scoffed at his disciples for believing him immortal. Yet a few centuries later the followers of Buddha had established one of the most obscrutinous tyrannies on Earth in the theocracy of Tibet. And as Russell points out:

> There is nothing accidental about this difference between a church and its founder. As soon as absolute truth is supposed to be contained in the sayings of a certain man, there is a body of experts to interpret his sayings, and these experts infallibly acquire power, since they hold the key to truth. They are in one respect worse than any other privileged caste since it is their business to expound an *unchanging* truth, revealed once and for all in utter perfection, so that they become necessarily opponents of all intellectual progress. The Church opposed Galileo and Darwin: in our own day it opposes Freud. The church, as everyone knows, opposed the abolition of slavery as long as they dared and, with a few well-advertised exceptions, they oppose at the present day, every movement towards economic justice.

No criticism of Christianity would be complete without a reference to its hatred of sexuality, so clearly articulated by Bunkum Buggeridge. Once again, Russell says it very well:

> Every boy is interested in trains. Suppose we told him that an interest in trains is wicked: suppose we kept his eyes bandaged whenever he was in a train or a railway station: suppose we never allowed the word 'train' to be mentioned in his presence and preserved an inpenetrable mystery as to the means by which he is transported from one place to another. The result would not be that he would cease to be interested in trains: on the contrary, he would become more interested than ever, but would have a morbid sense of sin, because his interest has been represented to him as improper. This is precisely what is done in the matter of sex: but as sex is more interesting than trains the results are worse. Almost every adult in the Christian community is more or less diseased nervously as a result of the taboo on sex knowledge when he or she was young. And the sense of sin which is thus artificially implanted is one of the causes of cruelty, timidity and stupidity in later life. There is no rational ground of any sort or kind for keeping a child ignorant of anything that he may wish to know, whether on sex or any other matter.

(Mind you, trains *are* indecent. All those funnels and tunnels.)

I can't imagine why I've written this. I suppose I was wearied by the people who write to the Editor confirming their undying belief in free speech while demanding my removal, my *exorcism* from these pages. At the same time I was growing weary of those letters full of fatuous theology and, worse still forgiveness. Christianity might forgive us atheists, but we're not ready to forgive Christianity.

The shame
of the white man

The scene is a conference room in the Sydney headquarters of what was then the Australian Council for the Arts. The *dramatis personae* include the scourge of private schools, Professor Karmel, the ever-popular Jean Battersby, Rex Connor's friend Alan Renouf, media godfather Oswin and John Menadue, the newly appointed head of the Prime Minister's Department. As well as these Public Service heavies, there's a score of scruffs like David Williamson and your tubby columnist. While at the far end of the table is some-one I haven't met before, an Aboriginal called Wandjuk Marika.

In any meeting there are political tensions and tactical manoeuvres, with what David Williamson called a 'sub-text' going on beneath the dialogue. That is, while the words are saying one thing, nuance is conveying another. And you know what David means as the long agenda is debated, point by point. (Two council colleagues express agreement on an issue, and emphasise the cordiality of their relationship. But everyone knows there's a tug-of-war going on, a battle for a piece of territory.)

197

Thus things proceed, with the usual mixture of formality and banter. Only Wandjuk takes no part in the discussions. For hour after hour he sits there, quiet and motionless. More and more I found myself looking at his black, broad-nosed face. There is no other word for it than beautiful. There's a quality of stillness, of self-containment, and the eyes are gentle and dreaming, almost feminine. Wandjuk wears a vivid band across his high forehead and, although a young man, has a white beard fringing an otherwise clean-shaven face. Reminding me of the ceremonial beards Egyptian pharoahs tied to their chins, it accentuates an undeniably aristocratic quality in this man from Arnhem Land.

It comes a time in the meeting for chairmen of the council's seven boards to report on their activities. One by one we say our piece. Finally it is Wandjuk's turn to speak for his people and he asks for permission to stand. And he tells of travelling to the National Gallery of Victoria, where he has seen his people's most sacred and secret paintings on public display. Although he speaks very quietly, it is clear that he is deeply distressed.

For Wandjuk is the guardian of the culture of the Riratjuna tribe, of its music, legend and painting. He was charged with great responsibility by his father Mawalan, on his death in Darwin hospital. 'You are my first son,' Mawalan said. 'Take my heart, my works, carry on.' And now he fights to protect his tribe's magic in an air-conditioned office block. 'It is very wrong. You must help me,' he says, searching our faces. 'These things must not be seen. If they are, my people will die.' This is said without dramatic emphasis which, of course, makes it all the more dramatic. The simple certainty of the statement hangs in the air and for the first time that day the room is utterly, eloquently silent. No one murmurs in private conversation. No one shuffles paper.

And you believe him. You know he is telling the truth, that unless these paintings and sacred objects are taken from the sight of women and we white heathens, his tribe-people *will* perish. For we're in the presence of an ancient and profound culture, where faith can work tragic miracles.

Now Wandjuk takes a plastic bag and tips its contents on to the table. A cheap printed tea towel, a cotton tablecloth. Both carry reproductions of bark paintings. They're the sort of things you might find in Coles or in souvenir shops selling toy koalas and mulga-wood ashtrays. With expressive hands, Wandjuk points at the various designs, but for a long moment cannot find words. Then they come, hurt and confused.

'This is my father's painting and this is my father's painting. This design of spears is my father's name. And here is my painting, and here is my painting. And all of these are my tribe's stories. The white man has stolen them. Who could do this? How could this happen?' It's hard to explain to Wandjuk that the manufacturer wouldn't have even thought about it. After all, they're only bark paintings by boongs. Not real paintings by proper artists. The tea-towel tycoon wouldn't realise that this is far more than a simple breach of copyright, far more than a minor act of vandalism. He couldn't know that this cheap cloth could tear the fabric of a unique and vulnerable society. 'For three years I've been unable to paint,' Wandjuk continues, 'I did not know why. Now I understand. These men have stolen my spirit.'

Tribal magic on a cheap tea towel. A clumsy, unintended blasphemy has robbed Wandjuk of his hereditary gifts. Each of us around the room shares the same sense of shame while, at the same time, recognising the incongruity of the situation. A Stone Age man trying to convince 20th century bureaucrats about black magic, about the occult forces of the dream time. And it is made all the more unreal by what I see shining on Wandjuk's wrist: the latest digital wrist watch, a tiny computer blinking out the hour, the minute, the second.

When we talk of living legends in our society, we're referring to mere celebrity. In contrast, the living legends of

Wandjuk's people involve the elements, the animals, the trees, the rocks. And such is the power of his advocacy that it is we, the whites around the table, who feel anachronistic. Suddenly it is Wandjuk's culture that seems enduring and substantial, while our society for all its might and technology and energy, is enervescent and unreal.

I have, on the book shelf above the typewriter, Angus and Robertson's *Australian Encyclopaedia,* printed in 1925. It refers to the way large tracts of Australia are 'infested' by Aboriginals.' Infested, for God's sake. The term used by 19th century bounty hunters like John Batman, who butchered Aborigines by the thousands, and by the squatters, who put arsenic in their flour and waterholes. Yet it's still a term that some Australians would feel appropriate. They say that behind every great fortune is a great crime. Surely the treatment of the Aborigines is the great crime behind the wealth of the Lucky Country.

And the guilt goes far beyond the cattlemen and the mining companies. It is a collective guilt involving the Rachmanite landlords of Redfern and the politicians who oppose progressive legislation. (I remember overhearing a prominent Country Party official on the steps of Parliament House in Canberra, as he sneered at the so-called Aboriginal Embassy below. 'They won't last the winter,' he said. 'The TB'll get them. Remind me to send them a flagon of metho.') And the guilt is shared by all of us who voted for Aboriginal dignity at a referendum that grows remote in time, and who've subsequently shrugged off any personal responsibility. Having washed our hands of the whole affair, we now wipe them on Wandjuk's tea towels.

Lament
for a lost lingo

Those who've enjoyed Cyril Pearl's *The Wild Men of Sydney* will remember, could not forget, the literary style of John Norton's *Truth* editorials. I think it's fair to say that even the most indignant of those in the *Age* pale with comparison beside an effort like the following, from a leader headed *Damn, Blast, Bloody*. In this, Norton gives an old adversary a blast with both barrels.

> Joseph Hector, you are a hidebound humbug, and a high faluting hypocrite . . . I always did regard you as a press-puffed nincompoop and a parson-boosted humbug . . . while your past connubial conduct makes you the concupiscent compere of some of those pornographic pulpiteers who have taken you under their pious parsonical protection.

After a work-out like that, Norton was ready to tackle a heavyweight contest. Thus he described Queen Victoria as 'this flabby, fat and flatulent-looking scion successor of a most ignoble line of Royal Georges', going on to describe her forebears and five fathers as madmen, lechers, bastards and blackguards. When retaliating against Norton, the *Daily Telegraph* echoed his alliterative style branding him 'this pugnacious, purposeful and political pygmy'.

If alliteration was popular, so was the use of flora and fauna as terms of abuse. Fowl language as it were. Consider the following transcript from a famous trial featuring John Norton and Richard Denis Meagher, the Honourable Member for Tweed.

> *Meagher:* You (expletive deleted) hound. You ought to be made to crawl out on your hands and knees.
> *Norton:* I never got my living in a brothel.
> *Meagher:* You scaly, scurvy contemptible viper!
> *Norton:* I never kept the door of a brothel or pulled the corks.
> *Meagher:* I'll show you up, you hound!
> *Norton:* You skunk. *You* show me up!
> *Meagher:* You're a skunk. Just as sick in body as you are in mind.

Norton: More damnable lies, you triple-tongued liar.
Meagher: You skunk, you scaly, scrofulous piece of carrion. You can't grow eyebrows, you wretched creature.
Norton: Look at his receding forehead, the champion criminal.
Meagher: (inaudible.)
Norton: Look at his prognathous jaw, his criminal lower lip, his retreating chin and gorilla mind, ha! ha! ha!
Meagher: You can't bluff me, you (expletive deleted) bit of carrion.
Norton: You're a beautiful bludger from a brothel to brag about dignity and decency.

A beautiful bludger from a brothel! Why don't you find things like that in *Reader's Digest* quotable quotes? Our court transcripts are the poorer for the passing of such impactive prose. Meanwhile, terms like rotten dingo are as dead as the dodo (and the drongo) when it comes to parliamentary Hansard while it is no longer considered proper to nickname a Prime Minister Toby Tosspot. Yes, our language has lost its kangaroo kick. Our invective is ineffective, and the prose of Press and Parliament just limps along.

Because the enfeeblement of language is an international problem, literary stylist Gore Vidal has tried hard to invent new dirty words. In the introduction of *Myron,* the salacious sequel to *Myra Breckenridge,* Vidal talks about a recent decision of the Supreme Court in regard to obscenity. Speaking for the majority of his fellow judges, Chief Justice Warren Burger conceded that no link had been found between the consumption of pornography and anti-social behaviour. Yet in the same breath he gave American communities the right to assume that such a connection existed if they so desired. In other words, as Vidal puts it: 'An outraged community may burn a witch even though, properly speaking, witches do not exist.' Faced with the fact that a word may be considered dirty in one district and quite acceptable in another, Vidal tried very hard to conform to both the letter and the spirit of the court's decision. Thus, in *Myron,* he replaced all those words which might have upset anyone, anywhere. 'Eliminate those "bad" or "dirty" words', said Gore, 'and you make the work "clean".'

Vidal decided to replace those usual words with some very respectable alternatives, the names of the high court judges who'd concurred in that majority decision. Thus Burger, Rehnquist and Powell were employed to describe parts of the anatomy that bring a blush to the cheeks in America's Chastity Bible Belts. As well, for other parts of the anatomy or for various sexual activities, Vidal appropriated such names as Father Morton Hill, SJ, and Mr Edward Keating, two of America's most formidable warriors in the cause of wowserism. 'I believe,' he concludes, 'that these substitutions are not only socially edifying and redemptive but tend to revive a language gone stale and inexact from too much burgering around with meanings.'

I think Vidal's ideal is impeccable and could, furthermore, be implemented on a global scale. Thus the efforts of members of the Festival of Light, the Mary Whitehouses and the chief censors like our own Mr Prowse could be immortalised. I'm sure they'd be delighted to see their surnames obliterating those unacceptable terms. Hiding them like fig leaves. Thus one could point one's prowse at the porcelain or take care to protect one's muggeridges. Come to think of it, I'd like to see the name Jennings used in some similar way, in honour of his family's continuing efforts to spread their brick veneerial disease from the suburbs into the Mornington Peninsula.

Moreover, I must admit to a certain disquiet by the tendency of slang and vernacular to borrow from sexual or excretory sources. Why should these pleasurable activities become terms of abuse? It suggests all sorts of sexual inhibitions and guilts on our part, not to mention poor potty training. On the other hand, on second thoughts, for all its colour and vitality, I cannot entirely approve of the epithets of Messrs

204

Norton and Meagher, given their origin in zoology. It's bad enough to be accused of sexism and racism without us bearing the burden of species-ism. Vipers, skunks, hounds and gorillas — not to mention dingoes — deserve a better Press.

How then to revive the language, to arm ourselves with words of spirit and impact? The matter is urgent given the tendency of young people to reduce their vocabulary to a handful of imports such as 'stoked', 'freaked', 'far out' and 'spunky'. While babies, gorillas and chimpanzees are being taught to talk and even form sentences (I'm told that some chimps have vocabularies of up to 150 words) the younger human being will soon be communicating, if you can call it that, in a series of grunts.

Well, Spike Milligan used to coin words and phrases, in the grand tradition of Edward Lear and Lewis Carrol. Those slithy toves were joined by useful phrases like 'ying-tong-iddle-I-po' and 'the dreaded lurgi'. So perhaps we should hold a contest, like we did for the national anthem, asking the creative among us to mint invective, to invent visionary vituperation. Or should we recycle old ribaldry? For make no mistake, given the brevity of our history and our lack of population, Australia has made a remarkable contribution to the genre. We might have failed at the Olympics, but when it comes to casting imaginative aspersions or to slinging matches we're hard to toss.

As I type, I have beside me the magnificent volume of Eric Partridge, *A Dictionary of Slang and Unconventional English.* This is the seventh edition of this major work of scholarship and contains almost 1600 pages of words and phrases coined in the streets, the pubs, the trenches. It is not the language of academy but the voice of every man, remarkable for its freshness and vivacity. And again and again, you find Mr Partridge identifying Australia as the source (which he may well have picked up at Toowoomba Grammar as a boy).

205

I've just opened a page at random, a column of BO words. Here we find grateful references to such unorthodoxlexicographs as Russell Drysdale, Jock Marshall, Vance Palmer and Lenny Lower, as well as to the Aboriginal language. There's Boob, an indigenous word for *faux pas;* Bodgoree, a word of Aboriginal origin meaning good, and Boodler, a term describing a politican on the make. We then have Boody, an Aboriginal word for snake, and Booey, a term describing nasal mucus or a non-cultured Australian domestic. Then follows such inspirations as Boofhead, Bookie, Boomer, Boong and Bootlaced, a Queensland term for branding. Further down we have Boots-and-all, Booze, Booze Artist and Booze-up, not to be confused with Boozle, a term used by Noel Coward to describe sexual intercourse.

And when I turn a few more pages, to the Ds, I find a surfeit of riches. It's true that words like Decko and Deener turn out to be foreign in origin, respectively Romany and French, but consider the others. The Australian has given hundreds of D-words to the English language, including the following . . .

Dag, Drongo, Dill, Darling Shower (for dust storm), Darlo (a diminutive for Darlinghurst), the Dead Cert, Digger, Dilly Bag, Ding-bat, Dinkum, Dinki-di, Dinky, the Dizzy Limit, the Donnybrook, Dosh, Droob, to Do In, Don, Donk, Dink, the Don (otherwise known as Braddles), Dodger, Dixie (those little buckets of ice cream) and the Dog Box. Not to forget Dog's Breakfast, Dog's Dinner, Dermo, Dim-Sim, and Ding-Dong (the inevitable nickname for anyone called Bell). We then have the Domain cocktail, a derro's drink made up of petrol and pepper, methylated spirits, boot polish and Flytox. Then comes Dora Grey, which is rhyming slang for tray or threepence, Duck-shoving and the Dust-up. Has any other vernacular ever shown such verbal, venal virtuousity? And there are twenty-four letters to go.

A while ago, Bill Wannan retired from active duty as a curator of our colloquialisms, a sort of one-man national trust trying to stem the tide of American imperialism, as relentless in its destruction of our idiom as their architecture has been of our cities. Wannan is dispirited by our willingness to yield to Americanisms, by the way we absorb their pop culture as if we were blotter. We've stood by and watched our dialect being razed to the ground, ready for the anonymity that goes by the name of redevelopment.

Of course, there is a clear alternative to the oral archaeology of a Partridge or a Wannan. We could employ the computer to give us new words, just as composers employ the Moog synthesizer for their music and artists play with the cathode tube. Indeed, the computer is already at work for capitalism, coming up with brandnames like Omo (now there's a case in point. We could use that as a substitute for poofter). What they do is programme their IBMs to come up with an alphabetical configuration for a product or for the name of the company, one that hasn't been used by any one else and that doesn't happen to mean something unspeakable in Hottentot or Paraguayan. And after a few minutes humming and whirring, the wretched machine will poke out a paper tongue and – lo and behold – you've Exxol for a multi-national oil company or Amatil to replace British Tobacco.

Perhaps we should organise a quick whip-around between journalists, politicans and pornographers so that we can programme a Honeywell to produce the oilifications suitable for a society approaching the 21st Century. Perhaps the machine might suggest we switch to numerals or to scientific equations. 'You can go and get $e = mc^2$.'

After all, it wasn't so many years ago that the typewriter developed a totally new way of swearing when it came up with $!%@. In fact, the only thing wrong with such typographic outbursts is that they're a little bit hard to pronounce. All in all, it's really a jennings of a problem, enough to give you a pain in the killens.

The journey to Never-Never land

As I have mentioned before, as a young child unable to believe in either God or his heaven, I became obsessed with mortality, with death. Because of this obsession I would read and re-read certain passages in books, trying to comprehend what it meant to die. Thus I was haunted by the description of Judy's death in *Seven Little Australians.*

> Judy grew quiet, and still more quiet. She shut her eyes so she could not see the gathering shadows.
>
> Meg's arms were round her, Meg's cheek was on her brow, Nell was holding her hands, Baby at her feet. Bunty's lips were on her hair. Like that they went with her right to the Great Valley, where there are no lights even for stumbling childish feet.
>
> The shadows were cold, and smote upon their hearts; they could feel the wind from the strange waters on their brows; but only she who is about to cross heard the low lapping of the waves.
>
> Just as her feet touched the water there was a figure in the doorway.

'Judy!' said a wild voice; and Pip brushed them aside and fell down beside her.

'Judy, Judy, Judy!'

The light flickered back in her eyes. She kissed him with pale lips, once, twice; she gave him both her hands, at her last smile.

Then the wind blew over them all, and with a little shudder, she slipped away.

Yes, it's an awful example of purple prose, of over-writing. Yet even now, despite my years and my cynicism, I'm still chilled by those metaphors of wind, waves and water. And my childhood reading gave me another metaphor for death that lingered in my memory. The crocodile that followed Captain Hook through the macabre and melancholy pages of *Peter Pan*. A crocodile that ticked because, as well as gobbling Captain Hook's hand, it had swallowed his clock. Not even the sight of an overweight woman playing Peter Pan in a Christmas panto ('she's the principal boy', was Mum's confusing answer to my inevitable question) could destroy my fascination with the character. For I feared growing up for the simple reason that it meant ageing and ageing meant dying. And by refusing to grow up, Peter Pan would live forever in Never-Never land. (There was an inevitable confusion in my mind between J M Barrie's Never-Never land and the place of the same name that Australian tenors sang about and Aeneas Gunn wrote about *The Little Bush Princess*. 'I'm riding to the Never-Never–Along a long wide road–A road that has no end.' My teachers told me that Never-Never land was true, that it was somewhere in the north of Australia. Curiouser and curiouser. It took me years to sort it all out.)

Now, looking back, I realise that Barrie shared my terror of death, shared my reluctance to grow up. And thanks to some stylish detective work by the English writer Alison Lurie, I've learnt that Barrie was much, much more than a cloying, maudlin, sentimental dramatist. He was a power-

210

ful novelist (his biographical books gave a stunning portrait of artistic corruption) and a genuinely tragic figure. For Peter Pan and Captain Hook turn out to be two parts of a tortured, almost schizophrenic self-portrait.

As Alison Lurie points out, the Victorians liked children to be seen and not heard, to be angelic and vulnerable. Thus it was common for angels to carry them off in novelettes and melodramas. Yet the early deaths of these kids were not viewed as entirely tragic. On the one hand they escaped worldly sin and suffering. On the other, they remained forever pure and happy in the Never-Never land above the Church of England spires.

> The room was dark, and when I heard the door shut and no sound come from the bed I was afraid, and I stood still . . . after a time I heard a listless voice . . . saying 'Is that you?' I thought it was the dead boy she was speaking to, and I said in a little lonely voice 'No, it's not him, it's just me.'

But although Barrie conceived Peter Pan while walking in the Kensington Gardens towards the end of Victoria's reign, those cultural conventions were not his inspiration. That lay in his own dark, terrible childhood. Until the age of six, Barrie was just an ordinary little boy, one of a large and impoverished family. It was his older brother, David Barrie, who seemed destined for greatness. His mother was convinced that he would win a scholarship to Edinburgh University and become a great preacher, 'the highest reward on Earth that any mother could hope for.' But David was killed the day before his fourteenth birthday. Stricken by the news, his mother stayed in bed from that day on, at first refusing to eat or to speak. When she found James crying on the stairs, his older sister, now responsible for the children and the chores, told him to go into his mother and remind her that she had 'another son'.

From that point on, Jamie almost lived in the dark room with his mother, trying to take David's place. And in the end he succeeded, becoming famous beyond his mother's wildest dreams. But at what a price; for James Barrie remained exactly as David had been on the day he died. Lurie writes:

> He became, and remained for the rest of his long life, a brilliant boy just short of puberty whose deepest attachment was to his mother. The resemblance was more than psychological: Barrie never grew to be more than five feet tall, and he was always extremely slight and youthful in appearance, with a thin, small voice. In photographs taken during his twenties and early thirties he looks like an adolescent boy wearing a false moustache and like those given to romantic crushes on pretty women, he was apparently incapable of physical love. His marriage at thirty-four to an actress in his first hit play was never consummated.

It was ten years after that marriage that Barrie met a charming family, the Davies, walking with their children and their nanny in Kensington Gardens. The tots made friends with Barrie's St Bernard, later to become the model for the canine nanny in Peter Pan. Soon Barrie and the Davies were inseparable, although Mr and Mrs Davies were in two minds about the situation. Mrs Davies became somewhat irritated with Jamie's soulful passion for her, while Mr Davies resented the author's success with his kids. For Barrie's imagination and storytelling soon captivated the Davies children.

Barrie developed a private fantasy for the kids and himself – all about Kensington Gardens. The hero was a Peter Pan who had flown from his nursery rather than grow up. Eventually these stories were published as part of a novel called *The Little White Bird*. Barrie was in his forties and the Davies children ranged from six years down. Barrie would take a holiday house near the Davies in Surrey over Christmas, adding complexities to the Peter Pan story, inventing games involving pirates, shipwrecks, Indians and desert

212

islands. He'd take photographs of the children acting out his plots and illustrated two copies of hand-bound volumes in this way. Arthur Davies showed his attitude to the goings-on by promptly losing his copy in the train.

Perhaps in retaliation, the portrait of the children's father in Peter Pan is less than flattering. Mr Darling was depicted as a coward, a bully, a hypocrite. For example, in one scene he pours foul-tasting medicine into the trusting dog's food bowl. When the family protested, Darling became hysterical.

Mr Darling: It was only a joke. Much good my wearing myself to the bone trying to be funny in this house.
Wendy (on her knees by the kennel): Father, Nanny is crying.
Mr Darling: Coddle her, nobody coddles me. Oh dear no. I am only the breadwinner. Why should I be coddled? Why, why, why?

Peter Pan went on to become the greatest success in the modern history of British theatre. And one of the marvellous stories Lurie digs up concerns its American producer, Charles Frohman, who was later to die in the sinking of the *Lusitania*. For as the ship went down he was heard to cry Peter Pan's curtain line in Act 3: 'To die will be an awfully great adventure.'

Barrie's identification with Peter Pan is very obvious. Captain James Hook shares not only his Christian name but his fear of death and his passion for cigars. And while he wants to possess Wendy, it's an asexual passion. (He just wants his fellow pirates to have a mother.) In this there's an echo of the resolute asexuality of Peter Pan who cried: 'You mustn't touch me, no one must ever touch me!' And Lurie points to a telling scene in the play script. After Pan has defeated Hook in their final duel 'the curtain rises to show Peter a very Napoleon on his ship. It must not rise again lest we see him on the poop in Hook's hat and cigars, and with a small iron claw.' According to Peter Davies, another Barrie expert, whenever the playwright was attracted by people he at once wanted to own them irrespective of their age or their sex. Thus assuming that Barrie wanted to own the Davies in 1904 it is possible to see Peter Pan as the innocent embodiment of this desire, and Captain Hook as the guilty one.

In the play, neither Peter Pan nor James Hook got their wish. But in real life, Barrie did finally possess the Davies. First of all, Mr Davies died of cancer, leaving Sylvia and the children in poverty. Barrie was able to step in and lavish luxuries and affection upon them. A little later, Sylvia Davies also died, leaving Barrie in charge of his five lost boys.

But reality soon invaded Never-Never land. No sooner had the boys stopped playing at pirates with Barrie than they were swept into World War I. George, the eldest, was killed in France and Peter was invalided home with severe shell shock.

As the surviving children had all grown up, Barrie was once again alone. Although still wealthy and famous, he developed a writer's cramp, both mentally and physically. Unable to work for several years, he suddenly found his right hand clenching into a claw, 'a late and uncanny imitation of Captain Hook'. Nonetheless Barrie taught himself to write with his left hand, turning out work of a distinctly sinister quality. Barrie remarked on this – that the writing of his right hand was far, far nicer. And you find an echo of this attitude in the traditional stage directions for *Peter Pan,* in which Barrie had the heroes entering from stage right and the villains from the left.

Mary Rose, Barrie's final play, is an eerie reworking of the Peter Pan theme, a Pan for melancholy grown-ups. There's no room for detail of the plot here. Suffice to say that Mary Rose combined Barrie's mother, his childless wife, his beloved Sylvia Davies. But she was also Barrie himself, someone who, like Peter Pan, was unable to grow old in an ageing world. And where that idea seemed so attractive in *Peter Pan,* in this final, mature work to be forever young is seen as a desolation, a tragedy. To quote Geduld, a third Barrie scholar: 'The message in Mary Rose can be expressed as the conviction that to attempt to hold back the clock, to deny the future for the sake of the past, is the pursuit of a fantasy that ultimately destroys the pursuer.'

In a world obsessed with youth, where a great percentage of the population abhor the idea of growing old (and to be thirty is seen to be old) the writings of Barrie have some relevance. So many people trying to stay young, to stay Peter Pans. So many older people trying to be young again. It's a desperate and pathetic situation. For my own part, I'm now reconciled to the ageing process and find it an interesting form of travel. On thinking back from the vantage point of my thirties to the oppressions of childhood, I wouldn't be a kid again for quids. And the strange thing is I've become almost fond of my ticking crocodile.

A few
departing words

Pete: 'Have you ever thought about death? Do you realise that each and every one of us needs must die?'
Dud: (After a stunned silence): 'Of course. But it's only half past four of a Wednesday afternoon.'

The Dagenham Dialogues

Call me necro-Phil. For where others collect stamps or match-box labels I collect last words, be they from the scaffold or the death bed.

Take Rabelais. 'I am going to seek the great, perhaps,' he said with a great sense of occasion. 'Draw the curtain. The farce is played out.' A century later the doubting Thomas Hobbes shuffled off this coil in much the same mood. 'Now I am about to take my last voyage,' he murmured. 'A great leap in the dark.' This was echoed by Henry Ward Beecher: 'Now comes the mystery'.

Nature has provided much inspiration to the departing. 'I go to see the Sun for the last time,' philosophized Rousseau, while Stonewall Jackson waxed even more lyrical with, 'Let us go over the river and sit in the shade of the trees'. 'The mountain is past,' murmured Frederick the Great. 'Now we shall get on better.'

The last words of royalty survive even when they lack distinction. It's just one of the perks of office. Take the characteristically brisk, Prussian remark of Wilhelm I: 'I haven't got time now to be tired.' 'I imagined it was more difficult to die,' said Louis XIV as they gave his pillows a final plumping. Far more spirited was the punch-line England's George II addressed at his dying wife, Caroline of Brandenburg-Ansbach. 'Don't look like a calf that has just had its throat cut,' snarled his Royal Highness, showing an impeccable death-bedside manner. Of the royals the only admirable sentiment was expressed by the much-maligned Charles II. Alone of all monarchs he was concerned for the well-being of a humble subject. 'Don't let poor Nelly starve.'

You possibly get a better perspective from the gallows

than you do from the throne. Thus one of the most concise pieces of existential philosophy came from our own Ned Kelly who, as they placed the knot behind his ear, shrugged and said 'such is life.' 'Death is but a little word,' said one Harry Bane on the scaffold in 1662, 'but it is a great work to die.' Commendably optimistic under similar circumstances, Jean Andre said, 'It will be but a momentary pang.'

But for those facing the firing squad, it was more of a momentary bang. Take Michel Ney, the most famous of Napoleon's marshals. Right to the end his upper lip was amazingly stiff. 'Soldiers!' he roared, 'Straight at my heart!' As for that great foe of slavery, John Brown, he was equally insistent on efficiency. So as to expedite his body a-moulderin' in the grave he was heard to say, 'I am ready at any time! Do not keep me waiting.' However, that pales into reticence beside the terminal oratory of Charles Guiteau, who was guillotined in 1882. 'Glory Hallelujah!' he shouted, 'I am going to the Lord! I'm calm! Ready! Go!' Whereupon he went.

Christianity must be a great comfort, as Oliver Cromwell was equally anxious to blast off. 'My desire is to make what haste I may to be gone.' In contrast, Cecil Rhodes was more concerned with his earthly schedule. 'So much to do,' he complained. 'So little time.' And while Benjamin Franklin found it a difficult business ('A dying man can do nothing easy'), Cotton Mather, famed advocate of puritanism and smallpox injections, was euphoric. 'Is this dying? Is this all? Is that what I feared when I prayed against a hard death! Oh, I can bear this! I can bear this! I can bear it!' All in all, I find that latter effort encouraging and hope to find it suitable for my own imminent demise. If not, I'll borrow that curtain speech of Oscar Wilde. According to a story that may well be apocryphal, he gazed disdainfully at some vulgar wallpaper and said, 'One of us will have to go.'

The most censored topic on this earth is not sex. It is death.

And Freud was wrong to see sexual torment at the heart of psychiatric illness. Had he looked deeper, he'd have seen the face of death. Indeed, the cacophony surrounding sex has served to distract us from the central fact of our existence – that we must die and die alone. Now, at last, those sexual taboos have been discarded and it's time to speak of the unspeakable.

Death has been my central theme, my obsession, in twenty-five years of writing, but as it's neither the most amusing nor popular of topics, one steers clear of it in newspaper columns or presents the subject in heavy disguise. It seems to me that the whole history of mankind has been a conspiracy to ignore it or a pathetic attempt to defeat it, with the prime motive of science, philosophy and most certainly of religion being to silence death's muffled drums. Not only has the church dismissed the reality of personal extinction, but every human effort seems directed at denying it. While our priests talked of life beyond the grave, the congregation tries to delay death's day of reckoning with everything from prayer to vitamin pills, from communion wafers to cosmetics.

But for all our elaborate theologies, cathedrals, rituals and self-deceptions, the most effective method of dealing with death has been out-and-out censorship. Like birth – that other parameter of mortality — death is hidden away behind closed doors, hospital screens and polite euphemisms. And as surely as the secrecy surrounding sex created pornography, the shrouding of death as a fact of life has created the pornography of violence. News reports of distant wars and disasters merely whet our appetites, so we crowd around road accidents, the Granville train crash, or queue for the simulated violence of the cinema.

I spoke of polite euphemisms. Consider the way we call death insurance life insurance and talk of 'passing on' or 'resting in peace'. We refuse to call a spade a spade, especially when it's held by a grave digger.

219

> 'There was a blast of trumpets
> The angel said come
> The gates of heaven opened
> And in walked mum.'

The words lack the grandeur of the Hallelujah Chorus, but they're singing the same song. They're telling us that we do not die. Yet no matter how we try to hush it up, death remains the skeleton in life's cupboard.

Alone of all living creatures we are cursed with a consciousness of our mortality. In the words of Dylan Thomas, we rage against the dying of the light. Some try to ward it off by the accumulation of wealth or power, but there's little evidence that this succeeds. Others hope their good works will enable them to survive, at least in the collective human memory, or through their children. Others try to show their courage through preliminary skirmishes with death behind the wheels of racing cars or dangling from mountains. Then there are those of us who try to cope with time by buying it in antique shops while, for another group of growing size, the fear of death is so crushing that they surrender to it, through suicide. And let's not forget those who transform their terror into art or even comedy. Confronted by the great practical joke of mortality, by cosmic absurdity, laughter is our saving grace.

Death also plays its role in love, which is, amongst other things, a shared awareness of mortality. Which is why the emotion is an almost intolerable mixture of joy and melancholy. You see it most clearly in parental love, so intensified by the enervescence of life. For even as you hold your children in your arms, time is taking them from you and you from them. Hence the poignant rituals of taking photographs for the family album or lighting those wretched candles on a birthday cake. No wonder 'happy birthday to you' is more of a dirge than a song.

Scientists are as discomforted by death as anybody. I'm

sure that the great scientific explorers, men like Galileo, were hoping to confirm the teaching of their religious faith, were hoping to prove what the priests had asserted. One can imagine the shock and dismay when their telescopes and microscopes made mockeries of the church's teaching. Now, centuries later, Galileo's followers wage an escalating war on death, trying to prolong life with everything from vaccines to transplants. And when all else fails, there's the chilling prospect of cryonics. Yes, a friendly technician will preserve you in liquid nitrogen, so that you can be defrosted at some future date. In the words of Professor Jean Rostand, 'We don't have long to wait before we shall know how to freeze the human organism without injuring it. When that happens, we shall have to replace cemeteries by dormitories, so that each of us may have the chance for immortality that the present state of knowledge seems to promise.'

And this is what makes our century different. On the one hand, death is becoming a more urgent preoccupation. What with our wars, famines and revolutions there's been so much of it of late. And with nuclear and environmental catastrophes and famines even more is waiting in the wings. On the other hand, we're running out of dreams and fantasies. (It's significant that for ten years more films have ended in death than in sunsets. Ever since *Elvira Madigan* the slow-motion demise of the young hero and heroine has become one of the dominant cinematic clichés, as the young try to romanticise their sense of peril, of dread.) Increasingly we see life for what it is, without the protection of what Nietzsche describes as the neurosis of religion.

So we turn to the scientist and ask him to save us, to give us an extra year or decade. We clamour for new hearts and plastic parts while millionaire businessmen follow in the pharaohs' footsteps and order those deep-freeze sarcophagi.

But at least the discussion about death is getting under way. 'We are a generation of the end and we should know that we are' wrote Paul Tillich, 'death has become powerful in our time. For nearly a century this was concealed in Western civilisation. We forgot that we are finite and we forgot the abyss of nothingness surrounding us.'

At last, people are facing up to the psychological, sociological, cultural and political implications of mortality. Already one feels that a greater sense of compassion and mutual responsibility is abroad in the world. Right through history men who believed in an eternal life were ready to mount bloody crusades and to butcher the heathen. In contrast, those who believed in mortality are less enthusiastic about killing or dying. I doubt that any force can bring people closer together than the thought of dying alone.